SHELLEY LEITH

Head to Soul

MAKEOVER

Helping Teen Girls Become Real In A Fake World

youth specialties

ZONDERVAN.com/
AUTHORTRACKER
follow your favorite authors

ZONDERVAN

Head-to-Soul Makeover Leader's Guide: Helping Teen Girls Become Real in a Fake World
Copyright © 2010 by Shelley R. Leith

YS Youth Specialties is a trademark of YOUTHWORKS!, INCORPORATED and is registered with the United States Patent and Trademark Office.

Requests for information should be addressed to:
Zondervan, *Grand Rapids, Michigan 49530*

ISBN 978-0-310-67041-4

Cover and interior design: SharpSeven Design

Printed in the United States of America

10 11 12 13 14 15 /DCI/ 23 22 21 20 19 18 17 16 15 14 13 12 11 10 9 8 7 6 5 4 3 2 1

CONTENTS

HELPING TEEN GIRLS BECOME REAL IN A FAKE WORLD

Character happens—whether you plan it or not. *Head-to-Soul Makeover: Helping Teen Girls Become Real in a Fake World* is a 10-week small group curriculum for girls in junior high and high school. This curriculum teaches the concepts found in *Character Makeover: 40 Days With a Life Coach to Create the Best You* by Katie Brazelton and Shelley Leith (Zondervan, 2009). The ten weekly studies in *Head-to-Soul Makeover* invite teen girls on the journey to proactively developing real character. While the material in the *Head-to-Soul Makeover* curriculum builds on the ideas explored in *Character Makeover*, the curriculum is entirely stand-alone and independent from the book.

This curriculum is specifically designed to address the root causes of the prevailing emotions of insecurity, anxiety, stress, irritability, and envy that can cripple girls during this critical stage of life as they are forming their adult identities. The key to overcoming such strongholds is to deepen the eight character qualities of Christlikeness. This is what makes you real in a fake world—becoming more and more like Christ. Using proven methods of group facilitation, combined with magazine-type self-quizzes, and themed with culturally-relevant reality shows, this upbeat curriculum takes personal proactive discipleship to a whole new level for the teen audience.

The *Head-to-Soul Makeover* study includes:

- Ten 60-minute lessons
- A weekly self-assessment quiz based on a reality television show
- Built-in discussion questions and interactive learning activities
- A Makeover Challenge exercise to deepen each character quality
- A Makeover Journal in which to record progress
- Accountability activities for three-person Makeover Teams

Each weekly "episode" uses a different television reality show as a metaphor to explore various character flaws that keep us from being like Christ. The "big reveal" identifies which aspect of a particular problem the participant needs to deal with the most. Then, your group looks into the Bible for the solutions.

HOW THIS STUDY WORKS

IT REFERS TO TELEVISION REALITY SHOWS

There is an abundance of reality shows on television where a coach helps someone change their decorating, eating habits, wardrobe, or even closets. In the same way that these shows feature people who work to change bad habits and make themselves more healthy/organized/ beautiful/appropriate on the outside, *Head-to-Soul Makeover* invites teenage girls to team up with the Holy Spirit to do some makeover work on the inside. Taking it a step further, this study uses popular reality television shows to illustrate the character qualities we are studying. It is important to note that referring to a particular reality show is neither an endorsement of the show nor an encouragement to watch it. In fact, the more odious shows, such as *My Super Sweet 16*, offer a vivid portrayal of some of the character flaws we must overcome in our lives—they give a clear picture of what we don't want to be! There is enough explanation of each show built into the curriculum that even those who have never seen a particular reality show will still feel like they can enjoy and appreciate the illustrations in the lesson. The Leader's Guide provides additional background information about each show in case you want to learn more.

IT HAS A BUILT-IN SCRIPT

The material that appears in bold type in this leader's guide is identical to the text featured in the *Head-to-Soul Makeover Participant's Guide*. It's written so you can read the text aloud to the group as if it were your script. Your introductions, your teaching setups, your explanation of Scriptures, your transitions between sections, and the discussion questions are all written in a conversational style so you can literally read it word-for-word to your group. It works well to have group members share the reading of the Scripture verses.

IT OFFERS WEEKLY QUIZZES

Each positive character quality overcomes a common character flaw or repeated area of defeat. The weekly quiz is a teaching tool that analyzes and breaks down the stronghold into its different aspects, and the results reveal which aspect of that stronghold needs the most work. Girls can also take each quiz online at www.headtosoulmakeover.com, where they can compare results with other participants across the nation. In the sections following the weekly quiz, the discussion moves away from the character flaws and shifts to the positive aspects of that week's character quality.

Here's a friendly leader-to-leader warning. These quizzes are not inerrant! If some girls in your group are ultra-analytical or overly literal, they may have a hard time mentally generalizing the situations enough to be able to choose a response that best matches their own. If the quizzes are frustrating to a participant, encourage her to see them as nothing more than a simple tool to help her discover which aspect of the character flaw she might want to focus on. **Try asking her:** *Would you agree that your score reflects the area you need to focus on the most?* If her quiz results point to the area where she *does* need the most work, then the purpose for the quiz has been served.

IT GIVES AN INTERACTIVE OBJECT LESSON

In order to help the kinesthetic learners in your group, a more interactive action segment is included in every lesson. This section may require advance preparation or bringing in items for each participant, so check the "Materials Needed" section at the beginning of each lesson when planning your meeting time. There's also an Idea Bulletin Board at www.headtosoulmakeover.com where leaders can share photos and experiences.

IT INCLUDES QUESTIONS TO DISCUSS

The key to being a successful facilitator of this study is to teach the material in the Bible lesson and help your group have a good discussion about it. **The entire text of the participant's guide is included in your leader's guide, printed in bold**, and many of the questions are followed by discussion tips to help you guide the group towards a healthy and productive discussion. **The discussion tips and leader guidelines are for your eyes only.**

IT OFFERS A CHOICE OF ACTION STEPS

Every week there is a Makeover Challenge, which invites each participant to choose an action step to help her work on developing that character quality. Participants choose the action step at the end of each lesson based on the results of the assessment they did earlier. If someone scored high in a particular area, she would probably be helped most by trying the Makeover Challenge designed to address that area. Participants can sign up to receive daily reminders at www.headtosoulmakeover.com.

THERE ARE BONUS CHALLENGES

In some weeks a Bonus Challenge is suggested. This type of challenge is one that the whole group is encouraged to try. Unlike the Makeover Challenge, it is not based on addressing one specific aspect of a particular problem. Rather, it is a general exercise which should benefit anyone in the group.

THERE'S A MAKEOVER JOURNAL

Each weekly "episode" ends with a space where participants are invited to write about what happens during the following week as they practice their Makeover Challenge and the Bonus Challenge. The journal includes specific prompts tailored to that week's challenge. Journal sections are also provided in the Leader's Guide so you can journal about your own progress too! If your group members prefer blogging, they can do so online at www.headtosoulmakeover.com.

HOW THE MAKEOVER TEAM WORKS

Makeover Teams are groups of three girls who meet together at the end of each study, and hopefully during the week. These teams talk together about the more personal aspects of the lesson—those areas where they might feel too vulnerable to talk in front of the larger group. Specifically, team members discuss results from the character assessment for that day, hold one another accountable for the action steps they chose, and pray for one another. Assign one member of the Makeover Team to be the Team Leader, and give her the responsibility of getting her team to connect during the week.

See Week 1 in the Leader's Guide for suggestions on forming Makeover Teams.

LEADERSHIP TIPS

TIMING

Each lesson is designed to take 60 minutes to go through, which includes the time needed to take the self-assessment quiz. But, with most groups, the discussion and the activities could easily stretch into an hour and a half or two hours, if you have that much time available.

Don't feel like you have to get through every question in the lesson. It is far more important to have a meaningful discussion about one or two topics than to get through all the discussion questions.

Some time-saving ideas:

If you have only 60 minutes and you're finding it difficult to fit everything in:

- Choose ahead of time which questions you want to concentrate on, and which you'll only ask if you have time.

- You could have the girls take the self-assessment before coming to the study, either in the books or online at www.headtosoulmakeover.com. (Be sure they print their results or send them to you.)

- Split your group into smaller groups for part of your discussion time. If your group includes more than eight girls, you will save time if you split up and allow smaller groups to discuss the questions on their own. Assign a discussion leader for each of your smaller groups to facilitate the discussion. (IDEA: These smaller groups could be the same as the Makeover Teams.)

GROUP HEALTH

In order to foster a healthy group, keep the following principles in mind as you lead:

Balance in participating

- You as the leader don't always have to be the first to share an answer to a question, nor do you always need to have the last word.

- Give participants time to think about a question before answering—don't rush to fill quiet moments with talking. Silences are not necessarily awkward—they provide safe zones where girls have time to formulate their thoughts. If they truly don't have any responses to a question, don't worry about it—just move on!

- Encourage participation, but don't legislate it. If group members don't feel pressured to always share, and if one or two are not dominating the discussion, everyone will feel more safe to be open and honest when they do speak up.

CONFIDENTIALITY

- **Everything shared in your group needs to remain confidential.** If a person's story is shared outside the group without her permission, the safety and openness of the group's interaction will be lost.

- Watch for gossip, and nip it in the bud. Participants can share stories from their own lives, but should not use examples from other people's lives if such examples reflect negatively on someone else's character.

VULNERABILITY

By its very nature a discussion about character flaws is threatening. Few people find it easy to share with a group of peers about their areas of greatest weakness and defeat! Encourage participants to be courageous and share anyway, because one individual's life experiences may be just what someone else in the room can relate to, or will be encouraged to hear. If you have the principles of balance in participating and confidentiality in place, vulnerability should readily follow. But, if your group is still hesitant to share, here is a great verse to give them "permission" to open up:

> *So now I am glad to boast about my weaknesses, so that the power of Christ may work through me. Since I know it is all for Christ's good, I am quite content with my weaknesses and with insults, hardships, persecutions, and calamities. For when I am weak, then I am strong. (2 Corinthians 12:9-10)*

If someone in your group is experiencing difficulties that are beyond your ability to support, you may need to privately encourage her to seek the counsel of your pastor or a counselor. You are not expected to be able to provide professional counseling.

STAY CONNECTED DURING THE WEEK

In a study such as this one, where participants are working hard at behavior modification, it is important to provide encouragement and reinforcement between meetings. Establish a habit of communicating with the girls during the week yourself, and of coaching the Makeover Team leaders to connect with their teammates. Some ways to enhance your midweek connections include:

- Collect and track prayer requests from your group members at your meeting, and pray together for one another at the close of your meetings.

- Follow up during the week on the prayer requests by emailing the prayer list to the group and reminding them to pray for one another.

- Review the week's Makeover Challenge in an email and encourage the girls to work on one area that week.

- Use texting, instant messaging, Twitter, or other electronic form of communication to communicate with the Makeover Team Leaders, reminding them to get their team members to connect with one another during the week. Give them ideas of questions they could ask their teammates or things they could do to model encouragement of one another.

Before we move into the first lesson, let's turn our attention to the introductory comments your group members are reading in their participant guide. As you read these opening remarks, pray for all the girls in your group, that your next ten weeks with them will help them experience genuine spiritual transformation.

WHY DO I NEED A HEAD-TO-SOUL MAKEOVER?

What a fake world we live in. Fake tans. Fake eyelashes. Fake teeth. Fake hair. Fake smiles. In such a plastic society, where pretending is normal and faking it is admired, it is all-too rare to come across a person who is real and genuine. Such a person is a breath of fresh air to be around, and we are drawn to her because she doesn't act stuck-up, doesn't put on masks, and doesn't try to be someone she's not.

But for many of us, it's hard to be real. There are things about us we'd like to hide or change. Maybe that's why makeover shows are so popular on television right now. We watch in fascination as a person gets a new chin or a different hairstyle, a wardrobe overhaul or a forced exercise regimen. We imagine what it would be like to get a head-to-toe makeover...how much more confident we'd feel, how popular we'd be, how we could relax and not worry about what others are thinking of us. We'd *finally* be able to be real.

Well, every single one of us needs a makeover. Not a head-to-toe makeover, but a head-to-soul makeover. And in this study, that's what we're all going to get! We'll change what's bothering us in our *heads*—things like insecurity, anxiety, stress, irritability, and envy—by working on character qualities in our *souls*—such as confidence, courage, self-control, patience, and contentment. The more we develop these character qualities, the more like Jesus Christ we will be—and that's what it takes to be truly real in a fake world.

Unlike reality-show makeovers that wash off with the next shower or start looking shabby over time, your Head-to-Soul Makeover has eternal benefits. When you join forces with God to overcome the character flaws that have been messing you up, you'll discover that God has created you to be a person of power, confidence, and hope. And you know what else happens as a side-benefit of a Head-to-Soul Makeover? You will become more genuine and real—and that is the most attractive type of person to be around!

So, are you ready to get started on the best makeover ever? Then, in the words of the *Extreme Makeover: Home Edition* team, "LET'S DO IT!"

EPISODE 1

WHAT**NOT**TO BE

This first lesson is based on the reality show *What Not to Wear*. To learn more about the show or watch episodes, go to the Web site:

http://tlc.discovery.com/fansites/whatnottowear/whatnottowear.html

SHOW SYNOPSIS

In the reality show *What Not to Wear*, participants are secretly nominated to appear on the show by their friends and relatives who think they could use a fashion makeover. Stacy and Clinton, the fashion coaches, spend the first day going through the person's entire wardrobe. They throw everything from the participant's closet into a big trash barrel—but not without first brutally critiquing her favorite outfits. Although their observations feel harsh, they are really trying to help the participant see herself from a different perspective and understand how unflattering her current wardrobe is.

Armed with $5,000 and shopping advice from Stacy and Clinton, the participant shops for two days, purchasing an entirely new wardrobe guided by new shopping rules her coaches have provided. After a hair makeover and a makeup lesson, she emerges with an entirely new look that suits her body type and enhances her self-esteem. Often the participant's external makeover is accompanied by an internal change in how she sees herself. The show closes with a big reveal where she astonishes a gathering of her friends and family with her beautiful new look.

MATERIALS NEEDED

- Butcher paper or tissue paper
- A T-shirt to trace around
- Fat magic markers (enough for each group member to have one or two colors)
- A large trash can (such as the tall barrel-type used outdoors)

PREPARATION

Using an actual T-shirt as a guide, use a magic marker to trace the outline of a shirt onto butcher paper or tissue paper, making enough paper T-shirts for all the members of your group, including yourself. To see photos and ideas from other groups, go to the Idea Bulletin Board at www.headtosoulmakeover.com.

CHAT ABOUT IT... 15 MINUTES

Start the lesson with the following ice-breaker question to get group members thinking about how certain reality shows help people transform parts of their lives:

In this study we're going to look at what it means to be *real* in a fake world. Each week, we're going to use a different *reality* television show to illustrate the character qualities that help us become more *real*. (Ha! Get the play on words? *Reality* show...becoming *real*?)

If you could be on a reality show—which one would you choose and why? You can choose one of these—or some other one!

- *The Biggest Loser*—where people compete to lose the most weight
- *What Not to Wear*—where people are coached to transform their fashion disasters
- *Extreme Makeover*—where people are transformed by plastic surgery
- *Trading Spaces*—where friends redecorate each other's rooms
- *Extreme Makeover: Home Edition*—where a family receives a whole new house

If your group members do not know one another, change this activity to a name game. Have the first person say, "My name is _____ and my favorite reality show is _____." Each additional speaker then has to repeat the name and favorite show of all the girls who have already spoken, and then add her own name and favorite reality show.

WHAT NOT TO BE

Today's lesson is based on the reality show *What Not to Wear*, except we're renaming it *What Not to Be*. For our show, we'll be focusing on character rather than clothes.

You'll probably want to ask the group if they've ever watched *What Not to Wear*. Even if most or all the girls have seen the show, it's best to read the show synopsis at the beginning of the lesson to make sure everyone has a good feel for what the show involves. After talking a little about the show itself, you can begin to help them make the connection between the actual show and our version—which focuses on letting go of ugly character traits rather than unfashionable clothing.

Girls nominated for *our* show, *What Not to Be*, have character flaws that make them irritating or unattractive. The coaches have ten weeks to give these girls "head-to-soul makeovers" that will help them become better people.

If you had to describe a teenage girl to be on the show, *What Not to Be*, what kinds of negative character qualities would she have? (Note: We're not naming people we'd nominate for the show—instead we're talking about character traits that need to be tossed in the trash can.

Be careful not to allow this discussion to degenerate into gossip or slander of a specific person. Keep the discussion on the hypothetical, or "I get really bugged by people who…" type of statements.

CHECK YOURSELF 10 MINUTES

Let's get personal now. For this episode you have nominated *yourself* to go on the show because you've noticed you keep having troubles with your parents, or in your relationships with your friends, or inside your head. You suspect you might have some character flaws, and you want to get help from a coach to become a more real and likeable person.

Let's begin this ten-week adventure by taking the *What Not to Be* Quiz. Taking the quiz is kind of like when the coaches on *What Not to Wear* go through a person's closet, identifying "fashion disaster" clothes. This will help you identify character flaws you need to throw in the garbage can—character qualities you should work on over the next ten weeks so that you can become more real.

Take the *What Not to Be Quiz* now or take it online at www.headtosoulmakeover.com.

Read the instructions aloud, and make sure girls read down each column and put a 1, 2, 3, 4, or 5 in every blank. The three columns don't mean anything—they are just a way to separate similar negative qualities to help get a more accurate result. You should also take the quiz yourself, and be willing to share your results.

To see how their results compare to the rest of the Head-to-Soul community, encourage your group members to try the online quiz at www.headtosoulmakeover.com. While they're there, they could take the next week's *Prideful Idol Tryout,* especially if you want to save time in your group meetings by having them take the assessments ahead of time. Have them bring a printout of their results, or email their results directly to you. Be sure they have your email address!

WHAT **NOT** TO BE QUIZ

For the following three sets of character flaws, rate each flaw from 1 to 5.

1 = I never or almost never feel or act like this

2 = I rarely feel or act like this

3 = I sometimes feel or act like this

4 = I often feel or act like this.

5 = I always or almost always feel or act like this.

SET 1

_____ A. Self-centered

_____ B. Insecure

_____ C. Fearful

_____ D. Obsessive

_____ E. Impatient

_____ F. Jealous

_____ G. Hate interruptions

_____ H. Difficulty finishing

SET 2

_____ A. Judgmental

_____ B. Low self-esteem

_____ C. Anxious

_____ D. Overly emotional

_____ E. Intolerant

_____ F. Rarely satisfied

_____ G. Trouble sharing things

_____ H. Easily discouraged

SET 3

_____ A. Perfectionistic

_____ B. Feel worthless

_____ C. Untruthful

_____ D. Stressed out

_____ E. Demanding

_____ F. Restless

_____ G. Greedy

_____ H. Avoid decisions

SCORE YOURSELF: Total your scores by adding up your 3 A's, your 3 B's, etc.

EXAMPLE: _3_ A. Self-centered + _4_ A. Judgmental + _2_ A. Perfectionistic = _9_ A's

REVEAL: *Circle your top 3 scores. These are 3 **character flaws** that you need to throw in the garbage can, and the **character quality** that will help you overcome them and become more genuine.*

A's _____ The character flaw of **Pride** is 'thrown away' by developing **Humility**.

B's _____ The character flaw of **Insecurity** is 'thrown away' by developing **Confidence**.

C's _____ The character flaw of **Fear** is 'thrown away' by developing **Courage**.

D's _____ The character flaw of **Anger** is 'thrown away' by developing **Self-Control**.

E's _____ The character flaw of **Impatience** is 'thrown away' by developing **Patience**.

F's _____ The character flaw of **Envy** is 'thrown away' by developing **Contentment**.

G's _____ The character flaw of **Greed** is 'thrown away' by developing **Generosity**.

H's _____ The character flaw of **Quitting** is 'thrown away' by developing **Perseverance**.

TRY IT OUT 10 MINUTES

For this activity, your leader will be passing paper T-shirts out to the entire group. Choose one of your top three character flaws and write it on your paper T-shirt. Think about why that flaw was one of your top three, and take turns sharing your thoughts with the rest of the group. Then come forward and toss your paper shirt in the trash can and say which positive character quality you're going to work on to help you "throw away" that flaw and become more genuine.

When everyone has finished scoring the quiz, distribute the paper T-shirts and markers, and ask each participant to look at her three highest-scoring flaws and choose one she's willing to share with the entire group. If a person's results are so even that there aren't three clear top scores, have her look at her highest scores and select three she thinks she needs to work on most.

Have each girl write the flaw she has chosen on her paper T-shirt. Then encourage group members to share their own thoughts about why they scored high is that particular area. Then have each girl take a turn bringing her paper T-shirt and throw it in the trash can, saying the statement from the scoring chart on the quiz: "I'm going to throw away _____ by developing _____."

What if the results are surprising? These character qualities may have some unexpected aspects to them. For instance, you may not think of humility as the character quality that would help overcome perfectionism. But, as we go through the study, we'll explore each of these qualities in more depth. If girls are surprised by any of their top scores, ask them to be sure to check it out when you do the lesson on that character quality, and decide at that time whether or not it's a fit.

And remind all the girls that there's room for each of us to grow in all these areas.

GREAT IDEA TO TRY

As the mentor of your group, it would be useful for you to know what each girl's top three character issues are. Fill in this chart by checking the boxes corresponding to each girl's top three, and refer to it as you go through the weekly studies, to help see where to reinforce and encourage your group members.

TOP THREE CHARACTER QUALITIES TO WORK ON

NAME	HUMILITY	CONFIDENCE	COURAGE	SELF-CONTROL	PATIENCE	CONTENTMENT	GENEROSITY	PERSEVERANCE

TALK IT OVER 15 MINUTES

Transition from the quiz results to the lesson by reading aloud the following section, which unpacks the title of the study, *Head-to-Soul Makeover: Becoming Real in a Fake World,* and ties it to the concept of discipleship.

Just in case you're thinking *What Not to Be* is all about making you popular, let's talk a little bit about the Most Real Person Ever. On *What Not to Wear*, when the coaches want to show their guest how to dress well, they demonstrate sample outfits on a mannequin. For our *What Not to Be* show, we have a living model who shows us what it means to live out these character qualities—Jesus.

Now, Jesus wasn't always popular. Not everyone approved of him. In fact, he alienated some people. So, why are we calling him the Most Real Person Ever? Because he possessed character qualities that pleased God, which meant he was genuine. He did what was right and loved people.

Can you think of stories from the Bible where Jesus exhibits the character qualities that make a person genuine?

A person who is genuine, or real, doesn't always appeal to everyone. If you have the courage to do the right thing, some people may feel alienated. When you reach out and love certain people, they may run away. But a genuine person treats others in ways that are caring. She doesn't change who she is to try to gain the approval of others. Jesus wasn't concerned about being popular. He was concerned about pleasing God, and that is a mark of true character.

So, on our show, *What Not to Be*, the goal is to "throw away" our character flaws and replace them with qualities that make us look and act like Jesus. The Bible calls this *process* discipleship, and it calls the *end result* being Christlike.

A MAKEOVER TAKES WORK

Have you ever been part of a team—such as a sports team, a musical group, or a drama production? Share the kinds of drills your coach or director has you do during practices.

Have you ever noticed that you don't improve your skills simply by joining the team? You improve your skills by practicing the disciplines, repeating the basics, and rehearsing the techniques. The same is true with improving your character. A *Head-to-Soul Makeover* doesn't happen just because you join the "Christian team." Take a look at these words from the apostle Paul:

> *Train yourself to be godly. For physical training is of some value, but godliness has value for all things, holding promise for both the present life and the life to come.* **(1 Timothy 4:7-8)**

According to this verse, what can we do to ourselves to achieve godliness (which is another word for being like Christ)?

The answer to this first question is found in the first two words of the Bible verse above: Train yourself. You could take this further by having the group discuss some ways we can spiritually train ourselves, such as studying the Bible together, going to church, having a daily quiet time, having an accountability partner, memorizing verses, etc.

How much value is there in becoming godly?

Again, the answer to this second question is found in those verses from 1 Timothy: Godliness has value for *all things*. You could go deeper by discussing what that looks like. For example, how would godliness be valuable in school? At your job? At home?

It is important to realize that godliness doesn't just happen. It is something we choose to work on and train into ourselves, which is what this *Head-to-Soul Makeover* is all about. Consider what Paul writes in Romans 5:3-4 (TLB):

> *We can rejoice, too, when we run into problems and trials, for we know that they are good for us; they help us learn to be patient. And patience develops strength of character in us and helps us trust God more each time we use it until finally our hope and faith are strong and steady.*

How is it that problems can make us rejoice?

Romans reminds us that problems help us develop strength of character, which in turn makes us strong and steady.

If strength of character makes us strong and steady, what does a life without strong character look like?

Answers here could be about feeling insecure, caving to peer pressure, or not standing up for one's faith. Look for opportunities to make connections between the girls' responses and the various character flaws you'll be considering during this study.

Can you think of a time when you didn't trust God and it made the situation worse?

Be prepared to share an example from your own life, such as a time you disobeyed God because you didn't think God's way would be fun, and then found out that your way didn't work.

Think again about your experiences as part of a team. How does being part of a group that's working together toward a shared goal help you achieve more than you could alone?

 # FORM A MAKEOVER TEAM 10 MINUTES

We're now going to form Makeover Teams of three girls each. These teams will stay together for the next ten weeks. Once you are with your new team, ask one another this question: *What were your top three character qualities to work on—and why?* **Send text messages, IMs, or emails to one another this week, offering encouragement and prayers to the other members of your team, such as "God, give Emily courage when she does her speech tomorrow." Be sure to exchange phone numbers, email addresses, and other contact info so you can connect during the week.**

Divide the girls into teams of three who will stay together for the whole study and act as accountability partners to one another. You may need to have some teams with either two or four girls if your numbers aren't evenly divisible by three. Each team should select a team leader to be the primary person you communicate with about the team. A good team leader would be a girl who loves activities such as writing notes and posting on Facebook, and who will be likely to return your phone calls and answer your emails! Here are several possible ways to determine who is on each team:

1. Let the girls choose their own teams and elect a leader who is good at communicating.

2. You decide which girls will be on teams together ahead of time, assigning older girls in the group to be team leaders.

3. To avoid cliques or complaints, divide the total number in your group by three, and then have the girls count off up to that number. (For example, if you have a group of fifteen, have the girls count off to five, then start over.) After everyone has a number, all the "ones" form a Makeover Team, all the "twos" are another team, etc. Have them choose a leader who is good at communicating.

Make a list for yourself of who is on each team, and who the team leader is, if applicable. If you have not already done so, collect complete contact information for the group members so you can communicate with them during the week.

Note that in the team time, the discussions get more personal than they do with the larger group. In the large group the girls are asked to choose just one character flaw they were willing to share. In their teams, they are encouraged to open up to one another and share all three of their highest scoring character flaws with one another.

Every week during the team time, the girls will choose a challenge to try for the following week. Before the larger group breaks up into teams each week, read through the Makeover Challenge section at the beginning of the upcoming week's journal together and answer any questions.

This first week everyone is assigned the same challenge. Encourage the Makeover Teams to discuss the question, exchange contact information, decide how they'll connect with one another during the week, and pray for one another about the work they're about to do on their character flaws. Then, bring the entire group back together, and close the meeting in prayer.

WHAT **NOT** TO BE
MAKEOVER JOURNAL • WEEK 1

 THIS WEEK'S MAKEOVER CHALLENGE

Start keeping your Makeover Journal. Begin your journal by listing the three character flaws you need to throw away and the related character qualities you need to work on. Throughout this week, record situations that come along that trigger one of the character flaws you ranked high on your quiz. (For instance: If fear is one of your flaws, and you're asked to give a speech in class that triggers fear in you, write that down!) Then look at the character quality that can help you deal with this problem (in this case, courage), and rejoice!

God has given you a chance to practice this quality and make it stronger it in your life! Want to blog it? Keep your Makeover Journal online at www.headtosoulmakeover.com.

MY TOP THREE CHARACTER FLAWS   THE CHARACTER QUALITIES I NEED

1. _____   _____

2. _____   _____

3. _____   _____

DATE: _____

WHAT WAS THE SITUATION? _____

_____

WHICH CHARACTER FLAW DID THIS SITUATION TRIGGER? _____

_____

HOW DID THE ASSOCIATED CHARACTER QUALITY HELP ME (OR NOT)?

_____

DATE: _____

WHAT WAS THE SITUATION? _____

_____

WHICH CHARACTER FLAW DID THIS SITUATION TRIGGER? _____

_____

HOW DID THE ASSOCIATED CHARACTER QUALITY HELP ME (OR NOT)?

_____

_____

DATE: _____

WHAT WAS THE SITUATION? _____

_____

WHICH CHARACTER FLAW DID THIS SITUATION TRIGGER? _____

_____

HOW DID THE ASSOCIATED CHARACTER QUALITY HELP ME (OR NOT)?

_____

_____

DATE: _____

WHAT WAS THE SITUATION? _____

_____

WHICH CHARACTER FLAW DID THIS SITUATION TRIGGER? _____

_____

HOW DID THE ASSOCIATED CHARACTER QUALITY HELP ME (OR NOT)?

_____

_____

DATE: _____

WHAT WAS THE SITUATION? _____
_____

WHICH CHARACTER FLAW DID THIS SITUATION TRIGGER? _____
_____

HOW DID THE ASSOCIATED CHARACTER QUALITY HELP ME (OR NOT)?
_____
_____

DATE: _____

WHAT WAS THE SITUATION? _____
_____

WHICH CHARACTER FLAW DID THIS SITUATION TRIGGER? _____
_____

HOW DID THE ASSOCIATED CHARACTER QUALITY HELP ME (OR NOT)?
_____
_____

DATE: _____

WHAT WAS THE SITUATION? _____
_____

WHICH CHARACTER FLAW DID THIS SITUATION TRIGGER? _____
_____

HOW DID THE ASSOCIATED CHARACTER QUALITY HELP ME (OR NOT)?
_____
_____

EPISODE 2

This lesson is based on the reality show, *American Idol*. To learn more about the show or watch episodes, go to the Web site: http://www.americanidol.com/.

SHOW SYNOPSIS

American Idol is a reality show that searches all over the country for unknown singers who compete for votes to become the next "American Idol." The show's title is based on our society's propensity to idolize its movie stars and recording artists. The process of locating contestants for the show involves a series of auditions all over the country, attended by thousands of hopefuls. The televised auditions are part of the appeal of the show: Viewers are treated to both the bizarre performers and the deluded ones who are unaware of how lacking in talent they really are. The frank assessment of the judges only adds to the entertainment value. Once the top 24 singers survive the auditions, millions of votes are cast by the television viewing audience each week, eliminating contestants until the person with the most votes is proclaimed the new American Idol and is given a cash prize and a recording contract.

MATERIALS NEEDED

- One hand mirror for each participant. Mirror should be about 5 inches in diameter. It works best and fastest if each girl has her own mirror to hold. If this is impractical, the experiment could be done using a large bathroom mirror, with groups of girls rotating through and trying the experiment while standing next to one another.

- One 3" x 3" square of paper for each participant (a Post-it Note works well)
- If any girls took the Prideful Idol Tryout online and sent you the results, print them out before the meeting and distribute them in the "Check Yourself" segment.

CHAT ABOUT IT 10 MINUTES

Start off the lesson with the following ice-breaker question to get the group recalling their experiences with their Makeover Challenge from last week. Encourage them to refer to examples they've written in their Makeover Journals to contribute to the discussion.

From your Makeover Journal, share something that happened this past week that gave you a chance to practice one of your character qualities.

This week, imagine yourself as a contestant in the singing competition reality show, *American Idol*. Thousands of hopefuls audition for this show, but many of the contestants are deluded about their musical abilities. Eventually, the field is narrowed to the top 12 performers, and telephone voting determines the "American Idol," who gets a recording contract and national fame.

Have you ever won a competition, election, or tryout? Did winning change you in any way? Can you think of any examples of people who were changed by fame or wealth or success?

Read the introduction to the four types of pride that sets up the self-assessment.

FOUR PRIDEFUL IDOLS

There are four types of pride that we can see among contestants on *American Idol*. And we may see the same kinds of pride among people we meet—or even in our own lives. Do you recognize any of these kinds of people?

"A prime example of a contestant with no talent is William Hung, from Season 5, who was arguably one of the worst singers to grace the *American Idol* audition stage. "I want to make music my living," said Hung, before he started singing and dancing badly to Ricky Martin's "She Bangs." After Simon said something derogatory about his performance, Hung said, "You know, I have no professional training of singing and dancing." Hung rapidly gained a cult following and has become more famous than many *American Idol* contestants."

FROM WIKIPEDIA, THE FREE ENCYCLOPEDIA

- **Idol 1 thinks too much of herself: This contestant has limited talent, but claims everyone tells her she's a great singer.**

- **Idol 2 thinks too little of herself: When this contestant is complimented, she puts herself down: "You really thought that was good? I don't think I sang very well."**

- **Idol 3 thinks too little of others: This contestant criticizes the judges and other contestants.**

- **Idol 4 ignores input from others: This contestant thinks she always knows best. When contestants ignore the judges' advice because they think they know better, they usually find themselves voted off the show.**

 # CHECK YOURSELF

Let's try out for our Character Makeover version of *American Idol,* **called** *Prideful Idol.* **In this tryout you'll discover which of the four Prideful Idols you are.**

Do the *Prideful Idol Tryout* now, either here or online at www.headtosoulmakeover.com.

Read the instructions aloud. You might want to mention that this "try-out" is one of the most difficult exercises of the whole study, because it focuses on such a hard problem to fix—our pride.

Take the self-assessment yourself, making mental adjustments to the situations for your own context, and be willing to share your results.

 **TRYOUT**

There are four types of pride seen in typical American Idol *contestants. Circle the number corresponding to how frequently you think you have exhibited each type of prideful attitude in the last few weeks.*

RARELY
ONCE IN A WHILE
SOMETIMES
FREQUENTLY

IDOL 1: I THINK TOO MUCH OF MYSELF

1 2 3 4   **Looking out for Number 1:** I seek to get the best for myself.

1 2 3 4   **Exaggerating:** I embellish the truth to make myself sound better.

1 2 3 4   **Name dropping:** Knowing important people makes me feel important.

1 2 3 4   **Self-centeredness:** I am insensitive to the needs of others. "It's all about me."

1 2 3 4   **Showing off:** I call attention to my possessions, abilities, or goodness.

IDOL 2: I THINK TOO LITTLE OF MYSELF

1 2 3 4   **False humility:** I point out my shortcomings, looking for reassurance.

1 2 3 4   **Undeserving:** I can't receive compliments, gifts, or help; I don't feel I deserve them.

1 2 3 4   **Overworking:** I do more than what is expected, looking for affirmation.

1 2 3 4   **Woe is me:** I often have some catastrophe I'm complaining about, looking for sympathy.

1 2 3 4   **Failure:** I feel I need to try hard because I haven't earned God's approval yet.

IDOL 3: I THINK TOO LITTLE OF OTHERS

1 2 3 4   **Argumentative:** When others speak, I focus on what I disagree with and argue about it.

1 2 3 4   **Critical:** I often find ways in which others don't meet my standards.

1 2 3 4   **Irritable:** I get annoyed easily and point out things that bother me.

1 2 3 4   **Judgmental:** I'm quick to assume the worst about people.

1 2 3 4   **Put-downs:** I intentionally belittle others with cutting or snubbing remarks.

RARELY
ONCE IN A WHILE
SOMETIMES
FREQUENTLY

IDOL 4: I IGNORE THE INPUT OF OTHERS

1 2 3 4   **Defensive:** If I'm caught in an error, I usually believe it wasn't my fault.

1 2 3 4   **Ignores suggestions:** I don't like to listen to advice. "You're not the boss of me."

1 2 3 4   **Isolated:** I reject help from others, preferring to go it alone.

1 2 3 4   **Refusal to change:** "This is just the way I am, so accept me."

1 2 3 4   **Unteachable:** I am closed to input or guidance. I have my act together.

TRYOUT RESULTS:

Idol 1: I Think Too Much of Myself   Total: _____

Idol 2: I Think Too Little of Myself   Total: _____

Idol 3: I Think Too Little of Others   Total: _____

Idol 4: I Ignore the Input of Others   Total: _____

TOTAL PRIDEFUL IDOL SCORE: _____

SCORING:

1-20   *You are a model of genuine humility.*

21-40   *You are learning to be more and more humble. Way to go!*

41-60   *Thank you for your honesty. That's the first step to humility!*

61-80   *Hmm! You have some work to do.*

When everyone has finished scoring their quizzes, ask the following questions.

Now that you have done the *Prideful Idol Tryout*, which type of Prideful Idol did you find most surprising to have on the list? Which of the Prideful Idols are the most difficult for you to be around? Which Prideful Idol total was highest for you?

For many people it is surprising to see "I think too little of myself" as a type of pride. Ask if they can guess why that is prideful. You'll explain the full answer in the lesson shortly.

Make sure the discussion of which types of prideful people are most difficult to be around stays general, and does not include names of people, or any gossip or slander.

TALK IT OVER 25 MINUTES

Transition from the quiz results to the lesson. Slowly and deliberately read the following section explaining the true meaning of humility, which ties back to the title of this study. Allow enough time for the concepts to sink in as you read.

THE *TRUE* AMERICAN IDOL

Let's turn our attention to the character quality that helps us be a true American Idol—not the kind you worship, or the kind who is prideful, but someone who is genuine and deeply attractive, a person people want to be around. This quality is humility. Now, you may be thinking humility is something it's not. Humility doesn't mean dressing ugly, letting everyone boss you around, or feeling worthless. Humility *does* mean thinking rightly about who you are in relation to God. Right thinking is realistic thinking—knowing your *real* strengths, your *true* weaknesses, your *genuine* talents, and your *real* worth. When you think *realistically* about yourself, you're "being a *real* person in a fake world"!

The scale below shows three kinds of thinking. On the right is boastful thinking, which is the most obvious form of pride. But, on the left end of the scale is false humility, the kind of thinking that says "everyone is better than me"—which is actually another form of pride. Such thinking is prideful because it's still all about getting people to focus on us, give us attention, and reassure us that we're not as pitiful as we say we are.

You may want to pause here to ask, "Okay, so how is 'I think too poorly of myself' really a form of pride?"

Humility is balanced in the middle. Humility means you have a right view of who you are and who you're not, and who God is—and that you just ain't him! When your eyes are always on yourself and whether you're better—or worse—than others, that's pride. When your eyes are on God, you can't help but be humble.

EVERYONE'S BETTER THAN ME!	I HAVE A RIGHT VIEW OF WHO I AM IN RELATION TO GOD.	I'M BETTER THAN EVERYONE!
FALSE HUMILITY = PRIDE	**HUMILITY**	**BOASTFUL = PRIDE**

INTRODUCING OUR "HUMBLE IDOL"

Do you know who Jesus named as the greatest person ever born? Well, it wasn't Moses of Red Sea and Ten Commandments fame; it wasn't David, who was a "man after God's own heart"; it wasn't Abraham, the father of the nation of Israel. Rather, it was the scruffy, wild-eyed hermit, John the Baptist, about whom Jesus said, "I tell you the truth: Among those born of women there has not arisen anyone greater than John the Baptist" (Matthew 11:11). Now, why was John the Baptist Jesus' top pick for World's Greatest Guy? Because he was humble. Let's see what we can learn about humility from our Humble Idol, John the Baptist.

1. A humble person has the right perspective about who she is. She says, "God is God—and I am not." Consider what John the Baptist once said:

> *"After me will come one more powerful than I, the thongs of whose sandals I am not worthy to stoop down and untie." (Mark 1:7)*

How does this statement show that John the Baptist was humble?

If you need to prompt answers to this question, refer back to our definition of humility, "Thinking rightly about who you are in relation to God."

Why isn't this false humility? What could you say about how you compare to Jesus that would show the right perspective on who you are?

If you need to prompt answers to this question, refer back to our definition of false humility, "Trying to get people to focus on us, give us attention, and reassure us that we're not as pitiful as we say we are."

2. A humble person directs people's attention to God. She says, "It's not about me." Take a look at our next passage:

> *The next day John was there again with two of his disciples. When he saw Jesus passing by, he said, "Look! The Lamb of God!" When the two disciples heard him say this, they followed Jesus.* **(John 1:35-37)**

How does this scene from John's life show that he was humble?

This answer comes from the section header: "A humble person directs people's attention to God,"—and (implied) away from herself.

How do you think he felt when his disciples left him? What can you say in certain situations to point people away from you and toward God?

Be prepared to share an answer from your own life here, to model this type of character. Have you ever been asked how you were able to handle a tough situation, and you credited God? Do you share the gospel when sending family update Christmas letters? Do you incorporate God, prayer, or Scripture into your conversations?

The final point gets to the conundrum about humility, and uses an experiment to demonstrate the way around it. Have mirrors and slips of paper ready to distribute to each girl as directed.

3. A humble person is not self-focused but God-focused. One problem with achieving humility is that it's impossible to develop it by working on it directly. The more you focus on humility, the more you are focusing on yourself, which is prideful. So how are you supposed to work on humility if working on it makes you prideful? Well, John the Baptist had a two-part formula:

> *"He must become greater, I must become less."*
> **(John 3:30)**

▶ TRY IT OUT   5 MINUTES

THE MIRROR EXPERIMENT

Here's how this works. *(Mirrors and small paper squares will be passed out to the group.)* **Look at your reflection in the mirror. Now, keep looking at yourself, but think about the second part of our formula for humility:** *"I must become less."* **So, try not to think about yourself right now... Is it possible?**

Allow the girls to answer, expressing their frustration with being unable to NOT think about themselves when trying not to think about themselves! Then have the girls pick up the Post-its in one hand, and have them keep their mirrors in their hands for the next step.

Now, while looking in your mirror, we're going to try the first part of the formula: *"He must become greater."* **Put the paper in front of the mirror, then move it closer and closer to your eyes until you can no longer see your reflection.**

You may want to demonstrate how they are to hold the mirror in one hand, away from their face a little, and the paper in the other hand, halfway between the mirror and their face. To see a photo of how this works, go to the Idea Bulletin Board at www.headtosoulmakeover.com.

After each girl has had a chance to try it, ask: "Did it work? Is the paper blocking your reflection?" Then invite them to put down the mirrors and lead them through the following progression of questions.

- *What just happened? Describe what you saw in the mirror as the paper got closer to your eyes.* (I couldn't see myself anymore—I only saw the paper.)

- *So, when working on the quality of humility, what happens when you try to start with the second half of the formula: "I must become less"?* (It doesn't work—I can't NOT think about myself when I'm trying to not think about myself.)

- *At the moment the paper blocked out your reflection, were you thinking of yourself or the paper?* (At that very moment? The paper.)

- *So, what happens to your thoughts about yourself when you start with "He must become greater"?* (I'm not thinking about myself anymore.)

- *What are some ways you can increase how much you focus on God?*

Collect their answers to this final question, and then lead into the God Hunt idea, which is a great way to help participants increase their focus on God.

CHECK IN WITH YOUR MAKEOVER TEAM
10 MINUTES

Read the following instructions for the Makeover Teams to reinforce what they should be doing together during their team time. Then, from the Makeover Journal section, read through the Makeover Challenge options and provide clarification as needed. Also read the instructions for the **Makeover Bonus Challenge: God Hunt** that all the girls should try. Have the group split into teams for their accountability discussion. After the teams have had their discussion and prayed together, bring the whole group together and close the meeting in prayer. If you want the girls to take next week's quiz ahead of time, remind them to do so.

Go back to your *Prideful Idol Tryout* and share with your team which type of pride tends to be the biggest problem for you and why. In your Makeover Journal for this week, choose your Makeover Challenge; share with your team which one you chose and why. Arrange to contact one another this week to check in on how you're doing on your God Hunt and the challenge you chose for the week.

**MAKEOVER JOURNAL
WEEK 2**

 # CHOOSE A MAKEOVER CHALLENGE

Choose a challenge based on what type of Prideful Idol you are, and write about how you do this week in your Makeover Journal. Want a daily reminder? Sign up at www.headtosoulmakeover.com.

If you scored highest in…	…try this Makeover Challenge to become more humble.
Idol 1. **I think too much of myself.**	☐ I will stop bragging, exaggerating, or showing off. I will do something nice for someone in secret, so I don't get noticed.
Idol 2. **I think too little of myself.**	☐ I will stop pointing out my shortcomings. I will practice simply saying "Thank you" when someone compliments me.
Idol 3. **I think too little of others.**	☐ I will stop being so judgmental. I will find something complimentary to say to a person whom I often find irritating.
Idol 4. **I ignore the input of others.**	☐ I will stop thinking I'm always right. I will say, "You're right, thank you for helping me," to someone who offers me advice.

MAKEOVER BONUS CHALLENGE: GO ON A GOD HUNT

To focus more on God and less on you, go on a God Hunt this week. Look for and then record in your Makeover Journal those moments when you see God show up in your day. Such times may include things you see in nature, interruptions, cool coincidences, delays, things that go right, frustrations, talks you have with people, answers to prayer—anytime you see signs of God's presence with you.

DATE: _____

Makeover Challenge

I tried my Makeover Challenge to become more humble, and here's what happened...

_____

_____

God Hunt

Today, I saw God show up when...

_____

_____

DATE: _____

Makeover Challenge

I tried my Makeover Challenge to become more humble, and here's what happened...

_____

_____

God Hunt

Today, I saw God show up when...

_____

_____

DATE: _____

Makeover Challenge

I tried my Makeover Challenge to become more humble, and here's what happened...

_____

_____

God Hunt

Today, I saw God show up when...

_____

_____

DATE: _____

Makeover Challenge

I tried my Makeover Challenge to become more humble, and here's what happened...

_____

_____

God Hunt

Today, I saw God show up when...

_____

_____

DATE: _____

Makeover Challenge

I tried my Makeover Challenge to become more humble, and here's what happened...

_____

_____

God Hunt

Today, I saw God show up when...

_____

_____

DATE: _____

Makeover Challenge

I tried my Makeover Challenge to become more humble, and here's what happened...

_____

_____

God Hunt

Today, I saw God show up when...

_____

_____

DATE: _____

Makeover Challenge

I tried my Makeover Challenge to become more humble, and here's what happened...

_____

_____

God Hunt

Today, I saw God show up when...

_____

_____

EPISODE 3

This lesson is based on the reality show *Don't Forget the Lyrics*. To learn more about the show or watch clips, go to the Web site: http://www.fox.com/dontforget/.

SHOW SYNOPSIS

Don't Forget the Lyrics! is a singing game show hosted by comedian Wayne Brady. The show's contestants compete to win one million dollars by correctly recalling and singing lyrics from ten songs. After every correct completion of a song lyric, the contestant has to make a decision, like the contestants do on *Who Wants to Be a Millionaire:* Will he or she continue to play for more money at the risk of losing what has already been earned, or quit and take home all the money earned so far?

The primary difference between *Don't Forget the Lyrics* and other music-based game shows is that artistic talent does not affect the contestants' chances of winning. In the words of one of their commercials, which is somehow fitting for this lesson about confidence, "You don't have to sing it well; you just have to sing it right."

MATERIALS NEEDED

- If any girls took the quiz online and sent you the results, print them out ahead of time and distribute the results in the "Check Yourself" segment.

CHAT ABOUT IT 10 MINUTES

Start off the lesson with the following ice-breaker question to get the group recalling their experiences with their Makeover Challenge from last week. Encourage them to refer to examples they've written in their Makeover Journals to contribute to the discussion.

From your Makeover Journal, share a time you saw God last week, and discuss whether or not the God Hunt helped you avoid focusing on yourself. How did you do on the Makeover Challenge you selected (doing something nice in secret, receiving a compliment with a simple "thank you," complimenting someone irritating, or being receptive to advice)?

This week we're talking about the game show *Don't Forget the Lyrics!* On this show, the beginning of a song is played, and then the contestant has to fill in the missing lyrics. Many of the competitors can't sing worth a darn, but that doesn't matter—they just have to know the words!

If you could choose any type of contest, what kind of competition would you be most likely to win?

This could be a fun discussion. The girls might decide they'd win a soccer contest, a scrambled-eggs-making contest, or even a "Bugging My Brother" contest!

Next, read the introduction to the concept of "self-talk" that sets up the self-assessment.

WHAT'S PLAYING ON YOUR IPOD?

The type of contest you said you'd be able to win signals an area where you feel *confident*. When you're engaged in that activity, you're probably telling yourself things like, "I can do this. I'm good at it. I enjoy this." We call this *positive self-talk*.

But sometimes we don't feel so confident. The messages in our minds may sound like this: "I'm a failure. I'll never get it. Why even try?" This is *negative self-talk*—and when we talk to ourselves like that, we feel insecure. And the more insecure we feel, the more we start faking it to cover up whatever we're insecure about!

You can choose your self-talk just like you choose what songs to put on your iPod. When you listen to a song over and over, you'll eventually memorize it word-for-word. You'll find the song running through your mind without even realizing it. Similarly, whatever self-talk you replay becomes a habit. If your self-talk is negative, you'll always feel insecure. But if you speak and think positively about yourself, you'll believe what you say to yourself—which will make you feel more confident!

 ## CHECK YOURSELF 10 MINUTES

Today, we're going to compete in a Head-to-Soul version of *Don't Forget the Lyrics!* We're calling it *Don't Replay the Lyrics!* Instead of challenging ourselves to remember song lyrics, we're going to fig- ure out what kind of self-talk is playing on the iPods of our minds.

Try *Don't Replay the Lyrics!* now. If you already took it online, refer to your printed results.

Slowly read the instructions aloud, emphasizing the iPod metaphor and explaining it further if necessary.

Take the self-assessment yourself, making mental adjustments to the answers for your own context, and be willing to share your results.

DON'T REPLAY THE LYRICS!

In Don't Replay the Lyrics! *instead of filling in song lyrics, you are completing thoughts with your typical self-talk. For each of the following situations, choose the self-talk that you tend to hear "replaying" on the iPod of your mind.*

1. **When I'm feeling insecure, I tell myself...**
    - ☐ God created me and loves me just the way I am. [I accept myself.]
    - ☐ My friends like me this way, so I must be okay. [I gauge my worth by what others seem to feel about me.]
    - ☐ I'm insecure, PLUS I'm lonely, PLUS I'm having a bad hair day. [When I feel insecure about one thing, I find additional reasons to feel even more insecure.]

2. **When I blow it, I tell myself...**
    - ☐ Everyone makes mistakes. Just admit it and try again. [I forgive myself.]
    - ☐ I hope no one noticed! If anyone saw this, I'm dead. [I get embarrassed.]
    - ☐ I am such a loser. [I call myself names.]

3. **When I have a big problem, I tell myself...**
    - ☐ I know I'll figure something out. [I'm usually positive.]
    - ☐ This isn't fair. I wish this weren't happening to me. Why me? [I usually question.]
    - ☐ There's no way I can get through this. I give up! [I usually despair.]

4. **When it comes to my choices, I tell myself...**
    - ☐ I've got to do what is right, even if my friends don't agree. [I'm independent.]
    - ☐ I'll do whatever my friends are doing. [I'm a copier.]
    - ☐ I do my best to try to make people happy, whatever it takes. [I'm a people-pleaser.]

5. **When I do something that's hurtful to a friend, I tell myself…**
   - ☐ I hate to hurt people. I'll have to apologize. [I own it.]
   - ☐ They're going to be so mad at me! They'll never forgive me. [I transfer my guilt to others and assume the worst.]
   - ☐ I'm going to beat myself up over this. I'll never forgive myself. [I punish myself.]

6. **When someone criticizes me, I tell myself…**
   - ☐ I'm still okay as a person, but maybe I need to listen and make some corrections. [I can find help in criticism.]
   - ☐ I feel like that person doesn't like me any more. [I take criticism as a personal attack.]
   - ☐ I am devastated! I know I disappoint people, and this just confirms it. [Criticism freaks me out.]

7. **When I'm new in a group, I tell myself…**
   - ☐ I wonder if there's anyone here I could get to know? [I reach out.]
   - ☐ Are they looking at me? Do they think I don't belong here? [I get self-conscious.]
   - ☐ This is so awkward! I wish I never came. I'll sit in the back and leave early. [I retreat.]

8. **When a friend genuinely compliments me, I tell myself…**
   - ☐ Wow! She's right! How awesome is that? [I receive compliments.]
   - ☐ That makes me uncomfortable. I don't like being the center of attention. [I feel awkward.]
   - ☐ She's so wrong. How could she possibly think that of me? [I reject compliments.]

9. **When I think about who I am, I tell myself…**
   - ☐ I have some great strengths, and some weaknesses that I'm working on. [I'm realistic.]
   - ☐ If I failed that day, I'm a failure. If I had a good day, I'm all right. [I flip-flop, based on circumstances.]
   - ☐ I am whatever my worst critics say I am. [I play their messages over and over in my mind.]

10. When I think about what I look like, I tell myself…

☐ There may be things I don't love about my looks, but I don't obsess about it. [My looks usually help me feel confident.]

☐ Mom says, "You have a great personality, dear!"—but that's not what guys go for. [My looks don't do my confidence any favors.]

☐ I wish I could hide my hair/complexion/weight/looks. [I obsess about my imperfections.]

11. When I think about being loved, I tell myself…

☐ God created me in his image and loved me enough to die for me. [I am lovable.]

☐ I feel best about myself when I have a boyfriend or best friend around. [I need affirmation.]

☐ I have a hard time believing I'm really loved for who I am. [I feel unworthy.]

12. When it comes to my past, I tell myself…

☐ What's past is past, and with God's help I can overcome my pain. [I let things go.]

☐ If my friends knew about my past, they'd think differently of me. [I cover things up.]

☐ My past feels like a trap. I'm stuck in patterns I can't change or get out of. [I feel imprisoned by my past and unable to change.]

13. When it comes to being different from my peers, I tell myself…

☐ I know my values and identity. What others believe or do doesn't really faze me. [I can stand alone.]

☐ It's important to have tolerance and avoid hurting people's feelings. [I don't speak out.]

☐ It would be better if I went along with what they're doing. [I conform.]

14. When I'm thinking about how I fit in with people, I tell myself…

☐ I feel relatively confident today, and on most days. [I am normal.]

☐ I scan the room and compare myself with everyone to see how I measure up. [I habitually rate myself.]

☐ Pretty much everyone I know is more confident/pretty/popular/successful/happy than I am. [I feel inferior.]

Confidence Scale

Shade in the number of boxes checked to see a visual scale of how confident, vulnerable, or insecure you are.

CONFIDENT: Total of all first boxes

1	2	3	4	5	6	7	8	9	10	11	12	13	14

UNCERTAIN: Total of all second boxes

1	2	3	4	5	6	7	8	9	10	11	12	13	14

INSECURE: Total of all third boxes

1	2	3	4	5	6	7	8	9	10	11	12	13	14

Key:
- **If you are Confident** in your self-talk, you reassure yourself, accept yourself, and embrace your strengths. You are real.
- **If you are Uncertain** in your self-talk, you question yourself, look to others for your cues, and rely on what other people say about you to establish how you feel about yourself.
- **If you are Insecure** in your self-talk, you are negative, you bash yourself, and call yourself names that make you feel defeated. You fake it in order to cover up your insecurities.

When everyone has finished scoring the quiz, invite some of your group members to share what the quiz said about how confident they are.

Some of you share from your Confidence Scale whether you are confident, uncertain, or insecure.

TRY IT OUT 5 MINUTES

To help participants really understand what self-talk is, ask them to complete the iPod exercise. The girls may need help identifying what they tell themselves at certain times in their lives. Refer back to some of the life situations in the *Don't Replay the Lyrics Quiz* to prompt them to think about their own self-talk, and have them complete at least three of the blanks.

Fill in some examples of the kind of self-talk you're replaying on the iPod of your mind.

I LOOK _____

I WISH _____

I FEEL _____

I'M NOT _____

I AM _____

_____

 # TALK IT OVER 25 MINUTES

Now transition from the quiz results to the lesson. Read the setup for the self-talk lesson, which establishes Philippians 4:8 as what God says our self-talk should be and then ties that idea back to our overall study theme of becoming real. Each of the eight statements from Philippians 4:8 is defined, illustrated with another verse, and then discussed. Have a different member of the group read each Scripture verse. Try not to dwell too long on one statement—allow enough time to talk about all eight.

CONFIDENCE-BUILDING LYRICS

Words that play over and over again in your mind are a primary influence on your confidence, so it's important that what you say about yourself agrees with what God says about you. So, what's so bad about self-talk that doesn't agree with what God thinks of you? Look at this progression of steps that can happen:

Step 1: You start with self-talk that conflicts with what God says about you. Your talk is full of negativity—statements like "I'm shameful," "I'm unworthy," "I'm worthless," "I'm ugly," "I'm a failure," "I'm unforgivable."

Step 2: You begin to believe your self-talk.

Step 3: Since you believe your self-talk, you feel you have to hide the parts of you that you feel ashamed of, so you wear masks, cover up, hide, pretend.

Step 4: You become more and more FAKE!

So, if you want to "become real in a fake world," you need to start over at Step 1 and change your self-talk to what God tells you to say to yourself. Read this verse from Philippians aloud together:

> *Whatever is true, whatever is noble, whatever is right, whatever is pure, whatever is lovely, whatever is admirable—if anything is excellent or praiseworthy—think about such things. (Philippians 4:8)*

If this list of qualities to focus on in yourself could become a list of songs, you could think of this as your "confidence playlist"! So let's look at each of these confidence-building tracks on our playlist, and see how to get real with ourselves and stop being fake.

This discussion about the things that make girls insecure will require an extra measure of *confidence* in order to share their areas of vulnerability with one another! Help your group give themselves permission to share by reassuring them of three important things:

1. What they share will be kept confidential within this group.

2. There will probably be someone else in the group who can relate to their life experiences and will be encouraged to hear their story.

3. Remind them that this is a perfect opportunity to practice last week's lesson on humility. Remind them of Paul's words:

    *So now **I am glad to boast about my weaknesses**, so that the power of Christ may work through me…For when I am weak, then I am strong.* (2 Corinthians 12:9-10)

▶ **WHATEVER IS TRUE: When you tell yourself whatever is true (or real), that means telling yourself what God says about you, instead of what someone else says.**

> Remember to have a different person read each Scripture verse.

> > *Then you will know the truth, and the truth will set you free. (John 8:32)*

What kinds of negative things do you say about yourself that are easily proven wrong (such as, "I can't do anything right")?

This area is a major one for many girls. They exaggerate ("Everything's going wrong today," or "My teacher hates me"), or generalize ("My life sucks," or "I'm a loser"), but upon closer analysis, their statements can't possibly be true.

Do you need to let go of something bothersome someone else said about you that just isn't true?

Here's a potential area of great hurt. If a girl was told, "You're just average," or "You're not beautiful," or "You were an accident," she may be holding on to that statement and embracing it as the true definition of who she is—even when the statement is false. Answers may not get that vulnerable, but be aware of this issue.

▶ **WHATEVER IS NOBLE: No matter how unworthy you may feel, God's love for you can't be shaken.**

> *"Though the mountains be shaken and the hills be removed, yet my unfailing love for you will not be shaken nor my covenant of peace be removed," says the Lord, who has compassion on you.* (Isaiah 54:10)

In what situations do you tell yourself you are worthless or unlovable? What can you find in yourself that is noble (noble means "worthy of honor or respect")?

Answers may be "surfacy" ("I get embarrassed when I walk into class late and feel like everyone's looking at me"), or they may get deep ("I never felt worthy of God's love because of my past"). Gauge how much honesty to ask of your group based on how safe the girls feel with one another. If it's a new group, allow them to stay on the surface. In answer to the second question, be prepared to affirm the girls by pointing out things "worthy of honor or respect" that you observe in them.

▶ **WHATEVER IS RIGHT: God promises to take care of you if you're mistreated by someone.**

> *Though my father and mother forsake me, the Lord will receive me.* (Psalm 27:10)

What kind of wrong has been done to you that has you telling yourself that your life isn't fair? What right thing can you start telling yourself about this situation instead?

Again, answers might be fairly superficial ("They switched my class schedule, and I don't like my new teacher," or "I didn't make the volleyball team") or it could get deeper ("My parents got divorced," or "My brother is in trouble all the time, and my parents ignore me"). Be prepared to help them restate what they tell themselves about their situations, so that they start focusing on what's right about it instead of what's unfair ("I might learn more from my new teacher," or "I might feel differently about my brother if I prayed for him and my parents").

▶ **WHATEVER IS PURE: Nothing you have done is beyond the reach of God's cleansing power.**

> *Long ago, even before he made the world, God chose us to be his very own through what Christ would do for us; he decided then to make us holy in his eyes, without a single fault—we who stand before him covered with his love.* **(Ephesians 1:4, TLB)**

What kinds of things make people feel impure, dirty, or unacceptable?

This question is purposely about "people" instead of about "you," so that the answers can stay impersonal, such as "if someone can't kick a bad habit," or "if a girl gets pregnant," or "when people get drunk and have a hangover." In addition to examples where people might feel impure or unacceptable because of things they've done, encourage them to think about situations where circumstances or the behavior of others might cause someone to feel unaccepted—such as someone who is made to feel she doesn't fit in because of her race or because she comes from a poor neighborhood.

Have you ever had a time when you told yourself you have done something that cannot be forgiven? Were you right?

Now we're moving into the ultra-personal. If your group is relationally new or untrusting, allow the answers to just be "yes" or "no" and move on. Refer them back to Ephesians 1:4 for the answer to "Were you right?"

▶ **WHATEVER IS LOVELY: God wants to replace your injured, broken, or ugly places with beauty.**

> *Those who look to him are radiant; their faces are never covered with shame.* **(Psalm 34:5)**

When you think about your appearance, is there anything about yourself that you would not necessarily call "lovely"? What does Psalm 34:5 say we can do to overcome our feelings of shame and look "radiant," or beautiful? Have you ever seen someone who has this quality of inner radiance that shines from inside? Describe what you think gives the person that radiance.

Now we're getting to an issue that is quite prevalent—body image. Be prepared to offer girls affirming statements so they can replace negative self-talk with meaningful positive self-talk regarding issues such as complexion, body shape, hair color or curliness, freckles, height, nose size, length of eyelashes—you name it.

▶ **WHATEVER IS ADMIRABLE: God gives you the power to do things you might not feel capable of accomplishing on your own.**

> *I have strength for all things in Christ who empowers me—I am ready for anything and equal to anything through him who infuses inner strength into me, that is, I am self-sufficient in Christ's sufficiency!* **(Philippians 4:13, AMP)**

In what kinds of situations do you feel like you can't lead the way, that you're afraid to speak from your heart, or that you need to shrink to the background? What can you tell yourself at times like that?

Possible answers to the first question could include being put on the spot about their faith, being asked to take on a new responsibility, or standing up to peer pressure. Refer them back to Philippians 4:13 to remind them what they can tell themselves in those times.

▶ **IF ANYTHING IS EXCELLENT: God's love and care for you proves your level of excellence in his eyes.**

> *Look at the ravens—they don't plant or harvest or have barns to store away their food, and yet they get along all right—for God feeds them. And you are far more valuable to him than any birds!* **(Luke 12:24, TLB)**

Do you feel like you're unworthy or worthless? Do you tell yourself that you're just average? If you could put yourself in God's place, what do you think he would tell you right now about your worth?

The first couple of questions are rhetorical. In answer to the final question, be prepared to offer some concepts from Scripture that will help them see themselves through God's eyes, such as "You're my child" (John 1:12), "I died for you" (1 Corinthians 6:19-20), "I adopted you" (Ephesians 1:3-8), "I planned you" (Psalm 139:16), "I created you" (Ephesians 2:10), "I have counted all your hairs" (Luke 12:7), "I see you" (1 Chronicles 28:9), "I hear you" (1 John 5:14), or "I have stored all your tears in a bottle" (Psalm 56:8).

▶ **OR PRAISEWORTHY: God made us acceptable, which results in praise to him.**

> *To the praise of his glorious grace, by which he has made us accepted in the Beloved.* **(Ephesians 1:6, KJV)**

When someone compliments you, do you feel you don't really deserve kindness, praise, or affirmation? When someone praises you, whom are they really praising? Why?

You can continue this line of questioning by asking, "Do you ever feel awkward when someone compliments you and you don't know how to respond?" "Does the fact that people are unconsciously affirming God's handiwork when they compliment you make it feel any different to you to receive praise?" "What would be a good response to a compliment?" (A cheesy thing to say would be, "All the glory goes to God." An uncheesy thing to say would be a simple "Thank you,"—which affirms the person giving the compliment.)

CHECK IN WITH YOUR MAKEOVER TEAM 10 MINUTES

Read the following instructions for the Makeover Teams to reinforce what they should be doing together during their team time. From the Makeover Journal section, read through the Makeover Challenge options. Encourage the teams to work together to come up with new self-talk statements and to write them on the iPod illustration. Give them ideas of how to practice positive self-talk this week. Have the group split into teams for their accountability discussion. After the teams have had their discussion and prayed together, bring the whole group back together and close the meeting in prayer. If you want the group to take next week's quiz ahead of time, remind them now.

Share with your team what you learned about how confident or insecure you are from *Don't Replay the Lyrics!* In this week's Makeover Journal, help one another come up with new self-talk statements and write them on your iPods. Arrange to connect with one another this week, and say your statements out loud together. It might feel silly, but just try it, and tell each other, "We are becoming real!"

 # CHOOSE A MAKEOVER CHALLENGE

Mark the three types of positive self-talk you need the most. These are the areas where you tend to "fake it" in order to cover up something. Write some new positive self-talk statements that you can play back on the iPod of your mind, using the three types of positive self-talk you selected. Say these things out loud to yourself at least once a day, and soon, instead of faking it, you'll be REAL! In your Makeover Journal, record what self-talk plays on the iPod of your mind when certain things happen in your day.

- ☐ **Whatever is true:** I need to let go of a lie someone said about me and believe God.

- ☐ **Whatever is noble:** I need to affirm that God loves me even when I feel embarrassed.

- ☐ **Whatever is right:** I need to remember God will take care of the wrong done to me.

- ☐ **Whatever is pure:** I need to declare that God says I am forgivable.

- ☐ **Whatever is lovely:** I need to see the beauty God has given me for my 'ashes.'

- ☐ **Whatever is admirable:** I need to claim God's power when I feel incapable.

- ☐ **If anything is excellent:** I need to state that I'm valuable when I feel average.

- ☐ **Or praiseworthy:** I need to thank God that I'm acceptable when I feel undeserving.

MY NEW POSITIVE SELF-TALK STATEMENTS

I LOOK _____

I WISH _____

I FEEL _____

I'M NOT _____

MENU

I AM _____

_____

DATE: _____

Today, if people heard the iPod of my mind, this is the self-talk they would have heard...

_____

_____

Here is a message from God I can remember to support my positive self-talk and replace any negative self-talk...

_____

_____

DATE: _____

Today, if people heard the iPod of my mind, this is the self-talk they would have heard...

_____

_____

Here is a message from God I can remember to support my positive self-talk and replace any negative self-talk...

_____

_____

DATE: _____

Today, if people heard the iPod of my mind, this is the self-talk they would have heard...

_____

_____

Here is a message from God I can remember to support my positive self-talk and replace any negative self-talk...

_____

_____

DATE: _____

Today, if people heard the iPod of my mind, this is the self-talk they would have heard...

_____

_____

Here is a message from God I can remember to support my positive self-talk and replace any negative self-talk...

_____

_____

DATE: _____

Today, if people heard the iPod of my mind, this is the self-talk they would have heard...

_____

_____

Here is a message from God I can remember to support my positive self-talk and replace any negative self-talk...

_____

_____

DATE: _____

Today, if people heard the iPod of my mind, this is the self-talk they would have heard...

_____

_____

Here is a message from God I can remember to support my positive self-talk and replace any negative self-talk...

_____

_____

DATE: _____

Today, if people heard the iPod of my mind, this is the self-talk they would have heard...

_____

_____

Here is a message from God I can remember to support my positive self-talk and replace any negative self-talk...

_____

_____

EPISODE 4

Fear or Faith factor

This lesson is based on the reality show, *Fear Factor*. To learn more about the show or watch episodes, go to the Web site: http://www.nbc.com/Fear_Factor/index.shtml.

SHOW SYNOPSIS

Fear Factor is a reality game show where contestants compete against one another by trying to complete a series of frightening stunts in order to win a cash prize. The first stunt is designed to physically test each contestant—such as jumping from the roof of one high building to the next, with the fastest people moving to the next round. The second stunt is meant to challenge the contestants mentally. It usually involves eating something revolting (such as a cockroach), or getting close to an animal which many people would find scary. Those who complete this stunt without chickening out move to the final round. The last stunt is an extreme-type stunt like you'd see in an action film, such as flipping a car or escaping from a sinking aircraft fuselage. The player who completes this round fastest wins the prize.

MATERIALS NEEDED

- At least 3 Bibles, one for each discussion group
- Print out any online results from this week's test.

CHAT ABOUT IT... 10 MINUTES

Start off the lesson with the following ice-breaker question to get the group recalling their experiences with their Makeover Challenge from last week. Encourage them to refer to examples they've written in their Makeover Journals to contribute to the discussion.

Last week we talked about replacing your negative self-talk with positive self-talk to build confidence and get more real with yourself.

Do you recall any moments this week when you caught yourself replaying an old negative message in your mind? Describe what happened.

This week we'll be considering *Fear Factor*, where contestants have to find the courage to face terrifying challenges to compete for a prize.

For you, which of the following actual stunts from the show *Fear Factor* would take the most courage?

1) Being locked in a box and covered with tarantulas

2) Eating wormy hotdogs and maggoty fried chicken

3) Leaping from one suspended beam to another, 20 stories in the air

4) Crouching for hours in a small, dark, enclosed septic tank with deafening sirens and occasional electric shocks

Read the introduction to the next section, which addresses the different reactions people have to threatening situations and sets up the self-assessment.

WHAT'S YOUR FEAR FACTOR?

People tend to react in a number of different ways to situations they find threatening—and that's true not just on reality shows but also in real life. Take a look at these three types of behavior that we're calling "fear factors":

- **STRESSING OUT** is when you can't stop worrying about something that might happen. *Stressing out takes over your thoughts and drains your energy.*

- **FREAKING OUT** is a common way of reacting when you feel threatened by people or situations you can't control. *Freaking out fills you with dread and causes you to shut down or lash out.*

- **HIDING OUT** is when you cover up your fear, which can take the form of denial, retreat, or lying. *Hiding out leads to deeper deception as you try to escape a consequence or cover your insecurity.*

 CHECK YOURSELF   10 MINUTES

In our Head-to-Soul Makeover version of the show, which we call *Fear or Faith Factor,* we're going to put you through a test to reveal the way you typically react in situations you find threatening.

Do the *Fear Finder Test* now, or use your online results from www.headtosoulmakeover.com

Read the instructions aloud slowly. Each situation is paired with a fear reaction...but the pairings are just to get them imagining themselves in a threatening situation. The girls should score themselves on every fear reaction, whether it's triggered by that type of situation or by something else. In other words, if someone often has the fear reaction of "I get very self-conscious," but she doesn't usually feel it when she's a visitor somewhere, she should still give herself a "3."

Take the self-assessment yourself, making mental adjustments to the situations for your own context, and be willing to share your results.

Fear or Faith factor

FEAR FINDER TEST

What is your fear factor? When you're in a tense situation, you experience some sort of fear reaction. Imagine yourself in the following situations, and look at a typical fear reaction you could have. Rate how much you experience each type of reaction:

0 = I never or hardly ever react this way.

1 = I react like this every once in a while.

2 = I sometimes react this way.

3 = This is how I tend to react most often.

LIST A: STRESSING OUT

Situation		Fear Reaction
Being a visitor	☐	I get very self-conscious. I'm afraid I'll look awkward and sit alone.
Going to an unsafe area	☐	I obsess about all the possible threats and danger.
Being too busy	☐	My worry escalates, especially about what I'm *not* getting done.
Trying to make friends	☐	I think too poorly of myself, so I imagine I'll be ignored or rejected.
Taking a risk	☐	I'm afraid to try because I might fail.
A painful past	☐	I have a hard time letting go of my past. It affects me to this day.
I have abandonment issues	☐	I don't trust. I expect to be left or hurt by anyone I trust.
I failed	☐	I am filled with regret; I keep punishing myself.

LIST B: FREAKING OUT

Situation		Fear Reaction
I feel insecure	☐	I make myself even more anxious by comparing myself to others.
Speaking in public	☐	I'm terrified I'll forget my words and make a fool of myself.
I push myself	☐	I can never relax—there's always something I'm not getting done.
I deal with pain	☐	I get pain-focused—it's hard to think about anything else.
I'm overwhelmed	☐	I don't sleep well. I feel anxious that I'm feeling anxious!
My life is changing	☐	I don't do well with change—it can push me over the edge.
I feel out of control	☐	The more uncontrollables in my life, the more headaches, stomach problems, and other physical ailments I develop.
I have phobias	☐	Fear of heights, fear of spiders, claustrophobia, etc.

LIST C: HIDING OUT

Situation	Fear Reaction
I said something I regret	☐ When discussing it later, I rephrase what I said to make it sound not so bad.
I don't meet expectations	☐ I hide my shortcomings in order to avoid criticism.
I failed	☐ I have a hard time apologizing and admitting I was wrong.
I succeeded	☐ I downplay it, afraid I'll have to live up to expectations I can't meet.
I embarrass easily	☐ I cover up my embarrassment so they won't whisper about me.
I made a mistake	☐ I fix the mistake and hide the evidence so no one will know.
The real me isn't worthy	☐ I hide who I really am so they'll accept me or like me.
I'm a Christian	☐ I avoid talking about my beliefs with non-Christians.

Scoring

Your highest score on the Fear Finder Test is the fear reaction you tend to use under stress.

List A Points:	**Stressing Out:** You react to fear by **obsessing** about what *might* happen.
List B Points:	**Freaking Out:** You react to fear with **apprehension** that can cripple you.
List C Points:	**Hiding Out:** You react to fear by **covering up** your true self.

When everyone has finished scoring the quiz, ask the following questions.

According to the *Fear Finder Test*, what is your most common reaction to threatening situations—stressing out, freaking out, or hiding out? Share a time when you reacted to stress using one of these "factors."

 ## TALK IT OVER 30 MINUTES

Transition from the quiz results to the lesson. Read the setup for the Faith Factor lesson, which looks at three Bible characters and how they reacted to threatening or stressful situations. Then split your group into three teams, according to their scores on the *Fear Finder Test*. If any girl's highest score is the same in two categories, place her on the team that needs more people. Make sure each team has at least one Bible so they can read the passages about their Bible character.

Each Bible character the teams are studying had a potential Fear Factor—a typical fearful response in that type of situation. Each person also had a Faith Factor—a God-powered response that provided the courage to meet the challenge. Each Faith Factor is further explained with a Faith Factor verse.

FAITH FACTORS

Just about every person in the Bible exhibited some type of fear factor when facing stressful situations. In response, each of them had to learn a "faith factor"—a spiritual tool (such as prayer, trust, or truth) they could use to combat their fears. Let's look at three of those people, and the faith factors they used to overcome their fears.

TRY IT OUT

According to the results of your *Fear Finder Test*, divide into three teams based on where you scored the highest: If you scored highest on List A, fear can make you one of the *Stressed-Out Sisters*; a high score on List B places you among the *Freaked-Out Friends*; and List C means you're part of the *Hide-Out Homegirls*. In your teams, discuss your Bible story, then come back together and teach the rest of the group what you learned about your Bible character's fear factor and faith factor.

TEAM 1: THE STRESSED-OUT SISTERS

Stress Situation: Someone Needs Help. One of the greatest stories of courage in the Bible is the dramatic story of Esther. The three central characters of the story are Esther, an orphan who hides her Jewish heritage and then wins a beauty contest that makes her queen; Haman, an officer of the court who plots to kill all Jews because of one man who would not bow to him; and Mordecai, the courageous Jew who refuses to bow, and whose stirring words challenge Esther to face her fears and take action to save the Jews from disaster.

After Queen Esther learns about Haman's plot to destroy the Jews, her Uncle Mordecai asks her to go before her husband, the king, and plead with him to save her people (See Esther 4:8). Facing this situation where someone desperately needs her help, Esther is also forced to face her own fears.

Think of a situation in your life where you know someone needs help. Maybe it's someone who's being bullied at school, a friend in a difficult home situation, or someone struggling due to poverty or racial tensions. What kind of courage would it take for you to take action and do something to help that person or that group of people?

Fear Factor: Stressing out. Esther's first reaction was to stress out. Her mind started playing out the bad things that might happen if she went in to see the king. (There was a law that said that any person who approached the king without first being called by him

could be put to death.) And the fact that the king hadn't asked to see Esther in a month made her even more stressed (See Esther 4:11).

What type of situation is most likely to trigger your fear reaction of stressing out?

Faith Factor: Prayer. When Esther realized she would die anyway if Haman's plot succeeded, she asked all the Jews to fast and pray with her for three days (See Esther 4:16). During this time, the Lord gave her the plan that eventually saved the Jews.

Here is what happens when we use the Faith Factor of prayer:

> *FAITH FACTOR VERSE: Do not be anxious about anything, but in everything, by prayer and petition, with thanksgiving, present your requests to God. And the peace of God, which transcends all understanding, will guard your hearts and your minds in Christ Jesus.* **(Philippians 4:6-7)**

What kinds of things that haven't happened yet do you worry about? When you're stressing out, how can this Faith Factor of prayer help you deal with it?

When your team gathers again with the rest of the group, explain to the group what stressing out is, what caused Esther to stress, and what faith factor she used to combat her worry. Share one example from your team's own experiences about how your faith factor verse can help you in a specific situation you have encountered.

When this team teaches the rest of the group, if they need help getting specific about worry situations, you could reinforce the concept that the things we worry about usually don't happen—such as worry about what people might say, worry about danger, worry about relationships, or worry about things going wrong on a test, speech, or project.

Have them restate Philippians 4:6-7 in their own words as the answer to worry.

TEAM 2: THE FREAKED-OUT FRIENDS

Stress Situation: Facing someone scary. David was the kid brother

of a group of not-so-kind big brothers. When he went to visit his brothers on the battlefield, not only did he end up facing Goliath alone, but he also had to face the criticism and ridicule of his own older brother (See 1 Samuel 17:28). Threatening enemies are scary, and so are overcritical relatives!

Is there anyone in your life who is threatening, bullying, or overcritical? What kind of fear reaction do you have around them?

Fear Factor: Freaking out. Actually, David himself never freaked out. It was his brothers and the entire Israelite army who were getting more and more anxious every day because of this terrifying giant they couldn't control, couldn't face, and couldn't get away from (See 1 Samuel 17:11, 24).

What type of situation is most likely to trigger your fear reaction of freaking out?

Faith Factor: Trust in God's Power. David declared the reason for his courage: "The Lord who rescued me from the paw of the lion and the paw of the bear will rescue me from the hand of this Philistine" (1 Samuel 17:37). David remembered God's power in the past, and knew God would help him in the present. Then he used his skill and killed Goliath with his slingshot. This could have been the time David wrote the psalm where we find this verse:

> FAITH FACTOR VERSE: *In God, whose word I praise—in God I trust and am not afraid. What can mere mortals do to me?* (Psalm 56:3-4)

When you're feeling so afraid that you're freaking out, how can the Faith Factor of trust in God's power help you have courage? What has God already given you that you can use when you face bullies, critics, or difficult situations?

When your team gathers again with the rest of the group, explain what freaking out is, what caused the Israelite army to freak out,

and what faith factor David used to combat fear. Share one example from your team about how your faith factor verse can help you in a specific situation you have encountered.

When this team is teaching the group, if they have trouble answering the question, "What has God already given you that you can use to face bullies, critics, or difficult situations?" refer them back to Psalm 56:3-4 to find what God has already provided. The answer is his Word. A possible follow-up question: "What stories or verse can you think of in God's Word that help you remember God's power when you're afraid?" Be prepared to share ideas, such as Joshua 1:9, Psalm 27:1, Psalm 34:7, or the story of Gideon from Judges 7.

TEAM 3: THE HIDE-OUT HOMEGIRLS

Stress Situation: Resisting peer pressure. Daniel was alone in his daily habit of praying. His jealous co-workers tried to use his faith against him by pressuring him to shift his worship from God to the king. They figured he'd refuse, so they made a law that he'd be forced to break in order to keep him from getting the promotion that they wanted for themselves (See Daniel 6:4-9).

Do you face any pressure from people to compromise in your behavior or deny what you believe? How do you deal with that?

Fear Factor: Hiding out. Daniel could have been tempted to hide his habit of praying by closing the windows or praying at night. Hiding your beliefs is a way of lying or deceiving others.

What type of situation is most likely to trigger your fear reaction of hiding out?

Faith Factor: Truth. Daniel faced his fear by living truly. He kept praying three times a day, in full view of the court (See Daniel 6:10). His open and honest practice of his faith got him a night with the lions, but God kept him safe and he was set free.

> *FAITH FACTOR VERSE: Then you will know the truth, and the truth will set you free. (John 8:32)*

Describe a situation in your life where you need to live truly or speak the truth.

This could be a situation where you cover up to protect yourself, where you're faking it to hide your true self, or where you're keeping a secret about something you or someone else is doing that is immoral, unethical, or dangerous.

When your team gathers again with the rest of the group, talk about what hiding out is, what could have caused Daniel to hide, and what faith factor he lived by instead. Share one example from your team about how your faith factor verse can help you in a specific situation you have encountered.

When this team is teaching the rest of the group, you may want to talk a little bit about the concept of when it's appropriate to keep a secret, and when it's not. Speaking the truth when someone has asked you to keep a secret about their immoral or dangerous behavior takes real courage. Another form of courage is speaking the truth when it feels like a little lie would save you from getting in trouble.

 # CHECK IN WITH YOUR MAKEOVER TEAM
10 MINUTES

Read the following instructions for the Makeover Teams to reinforce what they should be doing together during their team time. Then, from the Makeover Journal section, read through the Makeover Challenge options and read the instructions for the **Bonus Challenge: Turn Fears into Prayers.** Have the group split into teams for their accountability discussion. After the teams have had their discussions and prayed together, bring the group together and close the meeting in prayer.

Share with your team what your Fear Factor is and what kinds of situations cause you to have that kind of fear reaction. Go to your Makeover Journal for this week and choose your Makeover Challenge; share with your team which one you chose and why. Pray for one another about the situations in which you need more courage, and to remember to turn your own fear into prayers. Set a time to check in with one another this week and read one another at least one of the worry prayers you've written in your Makeover Journal.

MAKEOVER JOURNAL, WEEK 4

 # CHOOSE A MAKEOVER CHALLENGE

Choose a challenge based on which Fear Factor you want to overcome. Try the Bonus Challenge, too! Be sure to refer to the Faith Factor Verses to help you with your Makeover Challenge this week.

If my Fear Factor is...	...I will apply a Faith Factor and...
Stressing out	☐ **Befriend someone.** I will stop worrying about what people think of me and be friendly to a stranger I encounter during my day, or someone whom I've been avoiding because she or he seems to be so needy or scary.
Freaking out	☐ **Try an experience.** I will stop letting fear keep me from taking risks, and say "Yes!" to a new experience that I would normally avoid (such as helping at church, trying Persian food, or holding a snake!)
Hiding out	☐ **Keep a truth journal.** I will develop the courage to speak truthfully by keeping a list of the times I tell the truth, even when it might be tempting to mislead, cover up, or lie.

MAKEOVER BONUS CHALLENGE: TURN FEARS INTO PRAYERS

Turn your worried thoughts upward and tell them to God in prayer. Keep a list in your Makeover Journal this week of the fears you turned into prayers— you could even write out your prayers and go back and read them if you start worrying again. Share your prayers online in this week's Makeover Blog, and get ideas by reading other prayers at www.headtosoulmakeover.com.

DATE: _____

Makeover Challenge

Today, I overcame a Fear Factor when I showed courage by...

_____

_____

Turn Fears into Prayers

Dear Lord, today I'm worried about...

_____

_____

DATE: _____

Makeover Challenge

Today, I overcame a Fear Factor when I showed courage by...

_____

_____

Turn Fears into Prayers

Dear Lord, today I'm worried about...

_____

_____

DATE: _____

Makeover Challenge

Today, I overcame a Fear Factor when I showed courage by...

_____

_____

Turn Fears into Prayers

Dear Lord, today I'm worried about...

_____

_____

DATE: _____

Makeover Challenge

Today, I overcame a Fear Factor when I showed courage by...

_____

_____

Turn Fears into Prayers

Dear Lord, today I'm worried about...

_____

_____

DATE: _____

Makeover Challenge

Today, I overcame a Fear Factor when I showed courage by...

_____

_____

Turn Fears into Prayers

Dear Lord, today I'm worried about...

_____

_____

DATE: _____

Makeover Challenge

Today, I overcame a Fear Factor when I showed courage by...

_____

_____

Turn Fears into Prayers

Dear Lord, today I'm worried about...

_____

_____

DATE: _____

Makeover Challenge

Today, I overcame a Fear Factor when I showed courage by...

_____

_____

Turn Fears into Prayers

Dear Lord, today I'm worried about...

_____

_____

EPISODE 5

This lesson is based on the reality show, *The Biggest Loser*. To learn more about the show or watch episodes, go to the Web site: http://www.nbc.com/The_Biggest_Loser/.

SHOW SYNOPSIS

On *The Biggest Loser*, overweight contestants compete to win a cash prize by losing the highest percentage of their body weight through strenuous exercise and a rigorous diet. On every episode, contestants are faced with a temptation. For example, will they eat a fattening food in order to get a chance to call home? Will they skip a training session to win a cash prize? There are also reward challenges where individuals or teams compete in strenuous races (climbing piles of sand or jumping up to retrieve tennis balls) or tests of knowledge (estimating how many calories are in a dish or knowing seven principles of nutrition). The all-important weigh-in calculates what percentage of total body weight each team has lost. The team with the least weight loss meets to vote off one of their teammates, based on that week's performance in the temptation, the reward challenge and the weigh-in. After the contestants have spent three months at the ranch and four months at home continuing their regimen, the show culminates with a final weigh-in before a studio audience, and the contestant with the highest percentage of weight loss is proclaimed *The Biggest Loser*.

MATERIALS NEEDED
- Printed results from any students who "weighed in" online.

 # CHAT ABOUT IT 10 MINUTES

Start off the lesson with the following ice-breaker question to get the group recalling their experiences with their Makeover Challenge from last week. Encourage them to refer to examples they've written in their Makeover Journals to contribute to the discussion.

Last week's Courage Challenge may have pushed you to try something new. Share how you befriended someone, tried a new experience, or told the truth when tempted to lie. Did you try the Bonus Challenge of turning fears into prayers? Look back at the prayers you recorded in your Makeover Journal and share how that worked for you.

Dig down for some major self-control, because you're about to compete on *The Biggest Loser*. This weight-loss show is all about resisting temptation and exercising self-discipline. At the final weigh-in, the person who has done the best job of transforming his or her body with a new healthy lifestyle is the winner.

Let's talk about different temptations—which of these would be hardest for you to resist? Why?

(1) A refrigerator full of your favorite foods when you're trying to diet.

(2) Facebook messages from four friends when you're supposed to be studying.

(3) A group of girls gossiping about a person you have a story about.

(4) Buying something you love even though you have other things like it.

Read the introduction to the types of self-control we need to develop, which sets up the self-assessment.

WHAT DO YOU NEED TO LOSE?

Our version of *The Biggest Loser* **goes beyond losing weight. On our Head-to-Soul version of the show, becoming a** *Total Loser* **means exercising self-control and successfully losing your greatest area of temptation:**

- **LOSE THE MOUTH: If you are easily provoked or unkind, you need self-control over your speech.**

- **LOSE THE ATTITUDE: If you follow your impulses or give in to self-centeredness, you need to exercise self-control over your attitude.**

- **LOSE THE APPETITE: If a habit is controlling you and making you compromise, you need to exercise self-control over the appetites that drive you.**

 CHECK YOURSELF 10 MINUTES

Let's just make sure of one thing before we go on. This week, when we call ourselves "total losers," that's a good thing! We don't want to revert back to the negative self-talk and start calling ourselves "losers" as a way of putting ourselves down. This is the one time you can call yourself a "total loser" and it means something admirable!

When we go on *Total Loser,* **the first thing we have to do is "weigh in" to see what we have to lose.**

Do the *Total Loser Weigh-In* now, or weigh-in online at www.headtosoulmakeover.com.

Read the instructions aloud. This quiz utilizes the weight-loss metaphor in its terminology, so be prepared to clarify if necessary: "pounds" are points, "scales" are self-control topics, and the "weigh-in" is the scoring.

Take the self-assessment yourself, making mental adjustments to the situations for your own context, and be willing to share your results.

WEIGH-IN

What is the biggest thing you need to lose? Exercising self-control is the way to become a Total Loser, *whether that means losing hurtful words, selfish attitudes, or bad habits. Weigh yourself on three scales, giving each statement 0 to 4 pounds, in order to see where you need to become a* Total Loser.

0 pounds = I never have this issue

1 pounds = I hardly ever have this issue

2 pounds = I sometimes deal with this issue

3 pounds = I frequently struggle with this issue

4 pounds = I usually have a real problem with this issue

SCALE 1: LOSE THE MOUTH
(UNCONTROLLED WORDS AND EMOTIONS)

____ I tend to say hurtful things to people without even realizing it.

____ If I'm having a bad day, I take it out on my family or friends.

____ I enjoy a good gossip session with the girls.

____ I snap at people and get irritated easily.

____ I interrupt people and finish their sentences.

____ I get critical if I don't agree with what someone's doing.

____ I use swear words, or I use the name of God or Jesus as an expression.

____ I speak before I think, which gets me into trouble.

____ I tend to be judgmental, regularly jumping to conclusions or voicing a negative opinion.

____ I tend to overreact. My emotional levels go from one extreme to the other.

SCALE 2: LOSE THE ATTITUDE
(UNCONTROLLED IMPULSES AND SELF-CENTEREDNESS)

_____ I get stressed because I take on too much.

_____ I am a drama queen—I exaggerate how wonderful or terrible things are.

_____ I might disobey my parents if I think their rules don't make sense.

_____ I might break a rule at school if I think it doesn't make sense.

_____ I hold a grudge—it's hard for me to let go of a hurt.

_____ I tend to show off, especially if I accomplish something worth bragging about.

_____ I tend to complain—I can find something wrong with just about anything.

_____ I am a bit reckless—I act before I think, which gets me into trouble.

_____ I procrastinate, putting off things I don't feel like doing.

_____ I act religious, but I'm not sure I really buy into the whole God-thing.

SCALE 3: LOSE THE APPETITE (LACK OF WILLPOWER)

_____ I usually do whatever the group is doing and have a hard time resisting temptation.

_____ I consume too much caffeine, or diet pills, or energy drinks, or alcohol.

_____ I have trouble disciplining myself to work or do something I don't feel like doing.

_____ I am obsessed with exercise, or dieting, or my looks.

_____ I engage in more relaxation than I need (television, Facebook, sleep).

_____ I stay too long in relationships that drag me down.

_____ I do not have a balanced diet, and I eat to comfort myself.

_____ I don't have good work habits—I'm lazy, I get distracted, I go on Facebook instead of doing my homework.

_____ I have a habit (shopping, gambling, chat rooms, partying, etc.) I can't control.

_____ I "treat myself" too much (Starbucks, buying clothes, taking a break from work, etc.).

WEIGH-IN

Add your pounds on each scale to see where you need to be a Total Loser

Scale 1: 'Lose the Mouth' Total Pounds: _____

Scale 2: 'Lose the Attitude' Total Pounds: _____

Scale 3: 'Lose the Appetite' Total Pounds: _____

When everyone has finished scoring the quiz, ask the following questions.

When you "weighed in," in what area did you have the most "pounds" to lose? Can you think of anything that happened recently where you could have exercised more self-control?

 TALK IT OVER 30 MINUTES

Transition from the quiz results to the lesson. Read the setup of the Before & After Pictures lesson, which explains the connection between the reality show and what it's like to lack self-control. The Bible lesson for the most part uses Colossians 3 to show the contrast between a person without self-control (the "Before" Picture) and a person with self-control (the "After" Picture).

IMPORTANT NOTE: This lesson provides an opportunity for participants to receive "the most extreme makeover of all" by accepting Jesus Christ as Savior. It is only with him as Lord that we can truly be transformed into a new creation. Be prepared to invite your group members to pray to receive Christ at the conclusion of this lesson. For addtional resources to help you lead someone to Christ, go to www.headtosoulmakeover.com.

BEFORE AND AFTER PICTURES

The most captivating part of the reality show *The Biggest Loser* is when you get to see side-by-side comparisons of photos of contestants at the beginning of the show and at the end, 15 weeks later. The difference in the way a person looks after losing weight and getting healthier can be amazing.

Our *Total Loser* show invites us to an amazing change in our behavior. For example, a person who starts off with little or no self-control and "lets it all hang out" is not very attractive. She may say things like, "I always say what I think," or "What you see is what you get," or "I can't help the way I am." To this person, being "real" means being a real mess, because she just doesn't have the willpower to be any other way. But our show is all about losing the attitude and behaviors that weigh us down. Let's check out some 'Before' and 'After' pictures of the different types of "losers," as found in a few of Paul's letters in the New Testament.

 # TRY IT OUT

As we go through our lesson, we'll come back and fill in these 'Before' and 'After' pictures.

The 'Before' and 'After' pictures show a girl before she is dressed and after she has put on a beautiful ball gown. The ball gown is symbolic of her self-control makeover. It represents the spiritual clothing we put on to transform our old patterns into new ones. As you move through the lesson, remember to have group members take turns reading the Scriptures.

BEFORE   AFTER

LOSE THE MOUTH
"BEFORE" PICTURE

A person who needs to "lose the mouth" does not have a very pretty "Before" picture in this passage. Consider this description from Colossians where Paul suggests some traits worth losing:

> *But now is the time to get rid of anger, rage, malicious behavior, slander, and dirty language.* **(Colossians 3:8, NLT)**

When are you most likely to have trouble controlling your speech? (Think about how you speak when you're stressed, angry, hurt, tired, embarrassed, or frustrated.) On the "Before" picture, write in the type of speech you have trouble controlling (gossip, anger, criticism, crude language, etc.)

Have participants write something in the speech bubble on the "Before" picture. Be prepared to share what you've written on your picture as a way to help them think of their own answers.

"AFTER" PICTURE

Now let's take a look at the "After" picture. As this passage is read aloud, circle the action words that show how our speech can be transformed.

> *Let the words of Christ, in all their richness, live in your hearts and make you wise. Use his words to teach and counsel each other. Sing psalms and hymns and spiritual songs to God with thankful hearts. And whatever you do or say, let it be as a representative of the Lord Jesus.* **(Colossians 3:16-17, NLT)**

This passage suggests four things you can do to get control of your speech. What are they, and how can each one actually help you control your speech?

The four suggestions come directly from the passage:

1. **Let the words of Christ live in your hearts and make you wise.**
2. **Use his words to teach and counsel each other.**
3. **Sing psalms and hymns to God with thankful hearts.**
4. **Represent Jesus in whatever you do or say.**

Don't settle for surface answers to the "how" question. Get the group to envision situations where their words would normally be difficult to control, and ask, "What would the wise words of Christ be in that situation?" or "What words of Christ could you use to teach and counsel others?" or "How does thankful singing actually help you control your speech?" or "How does the idea of being Jesus' representative help you control your speech?"

On the "After" picture, write in one of these actions you'll use to control your speech.

Have participants write something in the speech bubble on the "After" picture. Be prepared to share what you've written on your picture as a way to help them think of their own answers.

LOSE THE ATTITUDE
"BEFORE" PICTURE

When you don't have self-control of your impulses or your self-centeredness, it can look pretty scary. Read this passage:

> *For people will love only themselves and their money. They will be boastful and proud, scoffing at God, disobedient to their parents, and ungrateful...They will be unloving and unforgiving; they will slander others and have no self-control...They will betray their friends, be reckless, be puffed up with pride, and love pleasure rather than God. They will act religious, but they will reject the power that could make them godly.*
> **(2 Timothy 3:2-5, NLT)**

Pick out the traits of a self-centered person from this passage—how many can you find?

Answers:

1. Loves only themselves
2. Loves money
3. Boastful
4. Proud
5. Scoffs at God
6. Disobedient to parents
7. Ungrateful
8. Unloving
9. Unforgiving
10. Slanders others
11. No self-control!!
12. Betrays their friends
13. Reckless
14. Puffed up with pride
15. Loves pleasure rather than God
16. Acts religious but rejects God's power

Select one of the traits in this "Before" description that you are most likely to show when you're acting self-centered, and describe how it looks on you.

This question asks the girls to imagine themselves from someone else's perspective, and think about how they probably appear to others—or how it feels for others—when they are acting self-centered.

Write it in the heart on your "Before" picture.

Have participants write something in the heart on the "Before" picture. The heart represents our attitudes. Be prepared to share what you've written in yours as a way to help them think of their own answers.

"AFTER" PICTURE

After you lose the attitude, you'll be "wearing" something different. Here's what you'll look like:

> *You must clothe yourselves with tenderhearted mercy, kindness, humility, gentleness, and patience. You must make allowance for each other's faults, and forgive anyone who offends you. Remember, the Lord forgave you, so you must forgive others. Above all, clothe yourselves with love, which binds all together in perfect harmony.* **(Colossians 3:12-14, NLT)**

What are the items in your new spiritual wardrobe that you'll be putting on for your "After" picture? How can these "clothes" help you lose your self-centered attitude?

Again, don't settle for surface answers. Dig deeper by asking them to think about specific self-centered actions they do, and explain how that item of spiritual clothing can help them "lose the attitude." (For instance: "If I put on the clothing of 'making allowances for other's faults,' then when I'm tempted to 'betray my friend' by complaining to everyone about how she keeps deserting me at lunch, instead I would try to understand why she does that and see it from her perspective."

Write one or more of these characteristics in the heart on your "After" picture.

Optional Salvation Discussion: Those 16 traits of a self-centered person are just as much of a choice to "put on" as these spiritual traits. But here's a distinction: The 2 Timothy passage describes people who live without the transforming power of Jesus, and the contrasting Colossians 3 passage is a portrait of a Christ-powered life. Be prepared to discuss the process of becoming a Christian, and receiving the forgiveness referred to in this Colossians passage.

Have participants write something in the heart on the 'After' picture. Be prepared to share what you've written in yours as a way to help them think of their own answers.

But don't stop this discussion yet! Be sure to emphasize what may be the most important and difficult part of this verse, "Remember the Lord forgave you, so you must forgive others." Ask if anyone has trouble with forgiving other people, and talk about how the concept of receiving Jesus' forgiveness for our own sins helps.

LOSE THE APPETITE
"BEFORE" PICTURE

Here's something that's tough to lose—your appetite for things that are bad for you...in other words, a bad habit. If a habit has power over you, here's what needs to happen:

> *So put to death the sinful, earthly things lurking within you. Have nothing to do with sexual immorality, impurity, lust, and evil desires. Don't be greedy, for a greedy person is an idolater. Because of these sins, the anger of God is coming.* **(Colossians 3:5-6, NLT)**

The first line of this passage uses some strong words to describe what you must do to lose your habit. What are they? (Say them with feeling!)

"Put to **death** the **sinful**, **earthly** things **lurking** within you!"

Why is it necessary to be so harsh with bad habits?

In other words, why do we have to take such strong measures with bad habits? Discuss the way habits are subconscious, how they are often linked to other things (such as when eating or shopping gets linked to comfort), and the fact that some habits are addictive.

Think of an appetite you have that's bad for you, and write it on your "Before" picture.

Have participants write something in the circle on the "Before" picture. It's positioned in the vicinity of the stomach, to represent "appetites." Be prepared to share what you've written in yours as a way to help them think of their own answers.

"AFTER" PICTURE

Again, being a "loser" means taking off old clothes and putting on a new wardrobe, but this time it's more like an extreme makeover. Look at the "After" picture:

> *You have stripped off your old evil nature and all its wicked deeds. Put on your new nature, and be renewed as you learn to know your Creator and become more like him. (Colossians 3:9-10)*

Tell the story of when you became clothed in your new nature. (That's another way of saying, "Tell how you became a Christian.")

Be prepared to share your own story of how you came to Christ. This could be a great time of growing closer as a group as you discover one another's spiritual journeys. This is also an opportunity for girls to disclose the fact that they might still be searching. You may need to spend extra time on this question and not even move on!

How has the presence of Christ in your life helped you "lose the appetite?"

If applicable, share a personal story about how God's power helped you overcome a habit.

Write that on your 'After' Picture.

Have participants write something in the circle on the 'After' picture. Be prepared to share what you've written in yours as a way to help them think of their own answers.

 # CHECK IN WITH YOUR MAKEOVER TEAM
10 MINUTES

Read the following instructions for the Makeover Teams to reinforce what they should be doing together during their team time. Read the Special Note, and be prepared to explain further how to become a Christian. Then, from the Makeover Journal section, read through the Makeover Challenge options and provide clarification as needed.

Have the group split into teams for the accountability discussion, but listen in to see if any of the teams need your involvement to pray with someone. After the teams have had their discussion and prayed together, bring the entire group together and close the meeting in prayer.

Go deeper with your Makeover Team by sharing a specific area from the *Total Loser Weigh-In* where you need more self-control. Go to your Makeover Journal for this week and choose your Makeover Challenge; share with your team which one you chose and why. Connect with one another this week and say, "You're a Total Loser!" Then, seriously cheer for the other members of your team as you all make progress in exercising self-control.

Special Note: *If you have not had the most extreme makeover of all, which is to invite Jesus Christ into your life so he can transform you into a new person, now is your chance! Your Makeover Team and your leader will pray with you.*

MAKEOVER JOURNAL
WEEK 5

CHOOSE A MAKEOVER CHALLENGE

Be a Total Loser by choosing the Makeover Challenge in the area where you need to lose the most and exercise the most self-control. Remember, the goal isn't to try to be someone you're not. Instead, the goal is to let go of any destructive behaviors that keep you from living out your true nature as a child of God. Keep track of your progress in your Makeover Journal.

If you scored highest in...	...try this Makeover Challenge to develop more self-control.
Lose the Mouth	☐ **Pray before you speak.** Try stopping and praying this verse before you say something you'll regret: "Set a guard over my mouth, Lord, keep watch over the door of my lips" (Psalm 141:3, TNIV).
Lose the Attitude	☐ **Resist a temptation.** Do the right thing even when you don't feel like it. This may mean obeying your parents, doing your homework, or not following the crowd.
Lose the Appetite	☐ **Start a new habit.** Replace your old habit with a new one, such as eating healthy, reading a chapter in Proverbs every day, or memorizing a verse to help you when you're tempted, like Romans 6:19.

DATE: _____

Today, I was a "Total Loser" when I exercised self-control by…

_____

_____

DATE: _____

Today, I was a "Total Loser" when I exercised self-control by…

_____

_____

DATE: _____

Today, I was a "Total Loser" when I exercised self-control by…

_____

_____

DATE: _____

Today, I was a "Total Loser" when I exercised self-control by…

_____

_____

DATE: _____

Today, I was a "Total Loser" when I exercised self-control by…

_____

_____

DATE: _____

Today, I was a "Total Loser" when I exercised self-control by…

_____

_____

DATE: _____

Today, I was a "Total Loser" when I exercised self-control by…

_____

_____

EPISODE 6

lifeswap

This lesson is based on the reality show, *WifeSwap*. To learn more about the show or watch episodes, go to the Web site: http://abc.go.com/primetime/wifeswap/.

SHOW SYNOPSIS

On the reality show, *WifeSwap*, two families exchange moms for two weeks. The two families are deliberately chosen for their extreme differences: highly regimented versus no rules at all; dramatically messy versus fastidiously neat; farmers that grow all their own food and home school versus an over-involved city family that rarely eats together; disengaged parents with rebellious kids versus a family that travels and performs together. Each wife leaves a house manual for the new wife, explaining the house rules and her role and duties in the family. The new wife must adhere to the rules and the lifestyle of the wife she is replacing for the first week of the swap. At the beginning of the second week, the family meets with the new wife for a "rules change ceremony." The new wife establishes her own rules, and the family must adhere to them, which usually involves drama and rebellion—often on the part of the husband! The show finishes with a face-to-face meeting between the two couples where they discuss what they learned and how they will change as a result of the previous two weeks.

MATERIALS NEEDED

- Deck of playing cards (enough cards to give each team of 3 girls about 10 cards)
- Printouts of any online results from this week's quiz.

CHAT ABOUT IT   10 MINUTES

Start off the lesson with the following ice-breaker question to get the group recalling their experiences with their Makeover Challenge from last week. Encourage them to refer to examples they've written in their Makeover Journals to contribute to the discussion.

See who was a *Total Loser* this past week by sharing stories about exercising self-control over your mouths, your attitudes, or your habits. Look over your Makeover Journal and share a time where you tried praying before speaking, resisting a temptation, or starting a new habit.

Today's reality show may be the most unnerving one of all. We're calling it *LifeSwap,* and it's based on *WifeSwap*—a show where two wives trade families for two weeks. The experience of living with people who are very different from you can be a supreme test of patience.

NOTE: The following profiles are of actual families that appeared on the show.

Which of the following real families from the show *WifeSwap* would be the most irritating for you to live with?

(A)   The Galvans, where a controlling mom picks which clothes everyone wears every day, sets a timer for how long the kids brush their teeth, inspects every room daily to make sure everything's perfectly clean, and listens in on everyone else's phone calls.

(B)   The Haigwoods, who raise their own food on their farm and eat it all raw (even the meat), don't believe in school (or home schooling), never buy anything new (they barter or buy used), and never eat in restaurants.

(C)   The Roys, whose home is out-of-control chaos: mountains of laundry, rooms where the floor can't be seen because of the mess, burping contests, public rudeness, frequent pranks, constant television, and absolutely no chores for anyone.

Read the introduction to the types of patience we need to develop, which sets up the self-assessment.

WHEN ARE YOU MOST IMPATIENT?

This week as a contestant on our show, *LifeSwap*, you'll be put into the living situation you find most irritating given your particular personality. It's a good thing we emphasized self-control last week, because you'll need to have control of your speech and your attitudes in order to exhibit patience toward others. *LifeSwap* gives you opportunities to exercise patience with...

- **IRRITATING PEOPLE: Let's face it. Even if you are the most self-controlled person in the world, some people are just irritating. It can take patience to understand and love certain people.**

- **PET PEEVES: We all have certain things that are guaranteed to annoy us. How you deal with your everyday annoyances tells a lot about how patient you are.**

- **WAITING: On the show *WifeSwap*, the women who switch homes must each live for a week with the other family's lifestyle before making any changes. It's not until the second half of the visit that the wives can make the rules everyone has to live by. If you find it hard to wait to get what you want, to see changes, or to gain control of a situation, then you need more patience.**

 CHECK YOURSELF 10 MINUTES

Okay. Brace yourself. *LifeSwap* is about to begin. Let's look at some irritating situations to find out where you most need to develop more patience.

Take The *LifeSwap Test* now or take the online version at www.headtosoulmakeover.com.

Read the instructions aloud. Each section of this survey has two parts: First, you select your biggest frustration (or write one in); then, you score yourself on a series of scales related to the frustration you chose.

Take the self-assessment yourself, making mental adjustments to the situations for your own context, and be willing to share your results.

TEST

If you had to do a LifeSwap and were forced to be with irritating people, endure your pet peeves, or wait for something you wanted, you would need a lot of patience. Select your biggest frustrations, then rate how you do at being patient with them.

IRRITATING PEOPLE

Check the type of person you'd find most irritating to have to live with for two days—or write in an idea of your own.

- ☐ A negative person who always complains
- ☐ A liar who is untrustworthy
- ☐ A person who always has a better story or a worse day than yours
- ☐ An incessant talker who never asks about you
- ☐ A bossy person who always has to be in charge
- ☐ Other_____

Oh no! That irritating person is in the family you are assigned for your LifeSwap! Circle the place on each scale that reflects how strongly you would lean toward one behavior or the other around that person.

1	2	3	4	5	6	7	8	9	10

I am irritable   I am kind

1	2	3	4	5	6	7	8	9	10

I judge that person   I try to understand why he or she is like that

| 1 | 2 | 3 | 4 | 5 | 6 | 7 | 8 | 9 | 10 |

I react in anger   I ignore small insults

| 1 | 2 | 3 | 4 | 5 | 6 | 7 | 8 | 9 | 10 |

I try to control that person   I try to love that person

| 1 | 2 | 3 | 4 | 5 | 6 | 7 | 8 | 9 | 10 |

I feel miserable when I think about that person   I have let go and moved on

PET PEEVES

Check the type of pet peeve that most annoys you—or write in your own idea.

- ☐ Being interrupted by a parent making you do a chore "right now"
- ☐ Losing something and having to look everywhere for it
- ☐ Cleaning up someone else's mess
- ☐ People who talk loudly on cell phones
- ☐ People who have annoying habits
- ☐ Other_____

The members of your LifeSwap family repeatedly do your most annoying pet peeve. Circle the place on each scale that reflects how strongly you would lean toward one reaction or the other.

| 1 | 2 | 3 | 4 | 5 | 6 | 7 | 8 | 9 | 10 |

I get frustrated quickly   I take a deep breath and chill

| 1 | 2 | 3 | 4 | 5 | 6 | 7 | 8 | 9 | 10 |

I get rather self-centered   I put others before myself

1	2	3	4	5	6	7	8	9	10

I complain, either aloud or to myself   I find something positive to say

1	2	3	4	5	6	7	8	9	10

I feel sorry for myself   I shrug my shoulders and forget it

1	2	3	4	5	6	7	8	9	10

I get angry when my expectations aren't met   I let go of my expectations

WAITING

In WifeSwap, *contestants must wait one week before implementing their way of doing things. In life, there are many kinds of waiting. Check the kind of waiting that is hardest for you— or write in your own idea.*

- ☐ Waiting for the day of a fun event you've been anticipating
- ☐ Being delayed or asked to stop moving forward on your plan
- ☐ Waiting for the right time to confront someone or say something you need to say
- ☐ Waiting to make a decision until you have evaluated it enough
- ☐ Waiting for your friend to forgive you and reconcile with you
- ☐ Other_____

Imagine the time you spend waiting in the situation you have circled. Circle the place on each scale that reflects how strongly you would lean toward one way of handling waiting or the other.

1	2	3	4	5	6	7	8	9	10

I get antsy and nervous   I release my need to control my schedule

1	2	3	4	5	6	7	8	9	10

I get depressed and feel far from God   I use the delay to pray

1	2	3	4	5	6	7	8	9	10

I act before I think   I think before I act

1	2	3	4	5	6	7	8	9	10

I do what feels good   I wait to make sure I'm doing what is right

1	2	3	4	5	6	7	8	9	10

I get confused and anxious   I wait until I have peace

LIFESWAP SCORE

Now, add up each section. Your lowest score is the area where you are the most impatient.

Irritating People _____   Pet Peeves _____   Waiting _____

When everyone has finished scoring the quiz, ask the following questions.

In what area of patience do you need to do the most work? What additional ideas did you write in?

TRY IT OUT   10 MINUTES

A TEST OF PATIENCE

Divide into teams and take two minutes to see which team can build the tallest house out of cards. After you're done, consider these questions:

Form teams of 3 or 4 girls. Give each team at least 10 playing cards, and tell them they all have to participate in building a house of cards. Their house won't "count" if one or more teammates just watch. The real goal isn't to build a house of cards, but to experience frustration—with the cards, and with one another! After two minutes affirm the team with the highest house of cards, then ask the following questions.

People work on problems in different ways. What did you observe about how others on your team tried to build a house of cards differently from you? Did you find yourself reacting with patience or impatience at these differences?

Be prepared to offer your observations here. The girls might need a little help perceiving how others worked differently from themselves. Make sure the answers are honest, yet tactful!

In what ways does a house of cards remind you of pet peeves?

Possible answers...the cards repeatedly did the same thing over and over. Just having them fall down once isn't that irritating, but when it happens again and again, that gets to you. After a while, it feels like they're out to get me. The cards are dumb—they don't do what I want them to.

What role does waiting play in building a house of cards?

Rushing never works. The slightest brush of air knocks them over. Moving too quickly and not thinking ahead makes your base unsteady, and your house falls over every time.

TALK IT OVER 20 MINUTES

Transition from the house of cards to the lesson. Read the setup of the Internal *LifeSwap*, which draws a correlation between the physical exchanging of families on *WifeSwap* and spiritually exchanging power sources to develop patience. The ideas for developing patience are called "rules," using the term from the *WifeSwap* show that describes how the families must conduct themselves. There are a total of nine rules with related Scriptures for you to read and discuss, so you'll need to keep things moving.

DO AN INTERNAL LIFESWAP

Instead of doing an external *LifeSwap* where we exchange families and endure situations that cause us impatience, we're going to try an internal *LifeSwap*, where we swap our impatience for God's patience. Like the second half of *WifeSwap*, in which the women get to set up new rules for the families they've been living with, *you* get to make the rules in your *LifeSwap*. Here are some new rules you can try to increase your patience with people, pet peeves and waiting.

LIFESWAP YOUR IRRITATION FOR GOD'S LOVE

If you're struggling to deal with people who irritate you, instead of lashing out at them, or gritting your teeth and hiding your feelings, try out these three new rules to help you have patience.

RULE 1: GIVE THEM UNDERSTANDING.

Try to understand people before getting irritated with them—you may discover an explanation for their behavior. *There's a connection between patience and understanding.*

NOTE: Patience is one of the character qualities that the teen girls surveyed said they needed most. Be aware of the prevalent need girls have for these "rules" as you lead them through this material.

> *Those who are patient have great understanding.*
> **(Proverbs 14:29)**

In what kinds of situations can **understanding** help you have patience with irritating people?

The concept here is that when you get to know a person, you may learn things about that person's childhood, family, health, or situation that can help explain the behavior that irritates you.

RULE 2: GIVE THEM A BREAK.

Even if you can't find any explanation for someone's behavior, over-look those faults by loving that person. *There's a connection be-tween patience and love.*

> *Be patient with each other, making allowance for*
> *each other's faults because of your love.*
> **(Ephesians 4:2, NLT)**

In what kinds of situations can **love** help you have patience with irritating people?

The point here is that patience isn't simply about what it does for you; it's also about loving because we're commanded to love. It can be very powerful to make the connection between patience and love—when I'm not showing patience, I'm not showing love!

RULE 3: GIVE THEM WHAT YOU'VE RECEIVED.

When you stop and think about it, God has had to exhibit far more patience with you over your lifetime than you have to show to the person you're irritated with at the moment. *There's a connection be-tween patience and mercy.*

> *But God had mercy on me so that Christ Jesus could*
> *use me as a prime example of his great patience with*
> *even the worst sinners.* **(1 Timothy 1:16)**

In what kinds of situations can **mercy** help you have patience with irritating people?

Another word for *mercy* is *grace*, which is God's undeserved favor. The very nature of patience is that you usually have to exercise it most with people who don't deserve it. This verse provides the power to do something that would be humanly impossible.

LIFESWAP YOUR ANNOYANCE FOR GOD'S SELFLESSNESS

Before we talk about the new rules for pet peeves, first let's find out what it is that annoys you.

What are your pet peeves? See how many things you can think of that trigger your impatience.

Get the girls to call out things that bug them—as many as they can think of. You're looking for short answers—sort of a fast-paced brainstorming session. The ideas they come up with will get them thinking of specific scenarios in which the following rules can be helpful.

So, when your pet peeves strike again, try these new rules (they're all from one verse in the "love chapter" of the Bible) to de-peeve those annoying 'pets'!

RULE 1: LET GO OF YOUR WAY.

Pet peeves are really nothing more than little moments of selfishness. Learn to let go of your agenda, your preferences, your expectations.

> *[Love is] never haughty or selfish or rude. Love does not demand its own way.* **(1 Corinthians 13:5a, TLB)**

Thinking back to your list of pet peeves, what is the link between selfishness and your pet peeves? How can you exercise patience instead?

RULE 2: LET GO OF YOUR PITY PARTY.

Impatient people tend to let pet peeves get to them quickly, especially when they're tired, frustrated, sick, or feeling sorry for themselves.

> *[Love] is not irritable or touchy.*
> **(1 Corinthians 13:5b, TLB)**

Are there certain situations in which you become irritable more quickly than at other times? How can you be patient in those times?

RULE 3: LET GO OF YOUR GRUDGE.

Sometimes pet peeves are best handled by not paying attention to them. Learn to let something slide, overlook an insult, or stop noticing every little thing someone does wrong.

> *[Love] does not hold grudges and will hardly even notice when others do it wrong.*
> **(1 Corinthians 13:5c, TLB)**

Can you think of a way to apply this verse to times when your pet peeves make you impatient?

LIFESWAP YOUR UNREST FOR GOD'S PEACE

Do you find it hard to wait? Here are your new rules to help you find peace while you're waiting.

This third type of patience—waiting—is needed to address presumptuousness, or thinking you know best (a typical teenage syndrome!). The concept of delayed gratification is more and more foreign in our microwave world. Be prepared to share your personal experiences in any of these areas, such as waiting on a decision of which college to attend until you had peace, waiting for a special purchase until you found the right thing, waiting to find the right spouse, waiting for marriage before having sex.

RULE 1: DON'T JUST DO SOMETHING—STAND THERE!

If you get presumptuous and assume God is late, you might decide to do something just to be doing *something!* You might make a snap decision, go with what feels good, or jump the gun and act even when the direction isn't clear.

> *God makes everything happen at the right time.*
> (Ecclesiastes 3:11, CEV)

In what situations have you felt like God was late? How does this verse—and this rule—help you not jump the gun?

RULE 2: DON'T FRET—PRAY.

Delays and roadblocks are there for a reason. Instead of stewing and fretting about what you should do, use the delay to pray. When you see the phrase "wait on the Lord," it usually means to pray while you wait!

> *Be still before the Lord and wait patiently for him; do not fret...* (Psalm 37:7)

How can prayer help you when you hit roadblocks along your way?

RULE 3: DON'T DECIDE IF YOU DON'T HAVE PEACE.

Don't steamroller over the roadblock or panic about your confusion. Invite God to stand there with you, and don't make a move until he releases you to do so by giving you peace.

> *For God is not a God of disorder, but of peace.*
> (1 Corinthians 14:33)

What kinds of delays have you experienced? How can this rule help you handle these situations?

CHECK IN WITH YOUR MAKEOVER TEAM

10 MINUTES

Read the following instructions for the Makeover Teams to reinforce what they should be doing together during their team time. Then, from the Makeover Journal section, read through the Makeover Challenge options and provide clarification as needed. Have the group split into teams for their accountability discussion. After the teams have had their discussion and prayed together, bring the entire group back together and close the meeting in prayer. If you want girls to do next week's quiz ahead of time, either online or in their books, remind them now.

Go back to your *LifeSwap* survey and share what makes you most impatient. Then choose the Makeover Challenge you'll work on in your journal this week. Share with your team which challenge you chose and why. Pray for one another about being patient. Set up a time and a way to connect during the week to encourage one another as you try out your internal *LifeSwap*. Try out the daily reminders at www.headtosoulmakeover.com to help you remember your *LifeSwap* challenge. This one could be the hardest of all!

MAKEOVER JOURNAL WEEK 6

CHOOSE A MAKEOVER CHALLENGE

Do an internal LifeSwap this week, choosing the Makeover Challenge that addresses the area where you most need to develop more patience. Refer back to the verses mentioned in the LifeSwap rules to help you. Keep track of your progress in your Makeover Journal.

If you have the hardest time with…	…try this Makeover Challenge to develop more patience.
Irritating People	☐ **Get to know the people who irritate you.** If you are habitually impatient with certain people, find out their interests, their pet peeves, the things that bring them joy or sadness. *LifeSwap* your irritation for God's love.
Pet Peeves	☐ **Don't sweat the little things…**and most of the things that bug us are little things. Purposefully let go of something that would normally annoy you. *LifeSwap* your annoyance for God's selflessness.
Waiting	☐ **Build in a pause.** Use the time to check in with God and see if he wants you to stay silent, to wait on your decision, or to pray until you have peace. *LifeSwap* your unrest for God's peace.

DATE: _____

Today, I did an internal *LifeSwap* and showed patience by…

_____

_____

DATE: _____

Today, I did an internal *LifeSwap* and showed patience by…

_____

_____

DATE: _____

Today, I did an internal *LifeSwap* and showed patience by…

_____

_____

DATE: _____

Today, I did an internal *LifeSwap* and showed patience by…

_____

_____

DATE: _____

Today, I did an internal *LifeSwap* and showed patience by…

_____

_____

DATE: _____

Today, I did an internal *LifeSwap* and showed patience by…

_____

_____

DATE: _____

Today, I did an internal *LifeSwap* and showed patience by…

_____

_____

My Superficial
SWEET 16

This lesson is based on the reality show, *My Super Sweet 16*. To learn more about the show or watch episodes, go to the Web site: http://www.mtv.com/ontv/dyn/sweet_16/series.jhtml.

SHOW SYNOPSIS

My Super Sweet 16 is a reality series documenting the celebration of the coming-of-age birthday parties of wealthy teenagers. The fascination of this show is in the juxtaposition of the lavish, permissive, self-indulgent event, on which hundreds of thousands of dollars are being spent, with the rude, demanding, and ungrateful attitude of the birthday girl. This show gives new meaning to the word "spoiled," as we see a meltdown when the new Mercedes is given at the wrong time, or a tantrum because the little sister's party dress makes her look hotter than the birthday girl, or sobbing because no one came out of the party tent to see her 'grand entrance' landing in the helicopter.

MATERIALS NEEDED

- **The Contentment Experiment:** Purses or bags from your own closet; one purse per participant. Include fancy purses, evening clutches, plain satchels, canvas carry-alls, even backpacks or fanny packs. You could adapt this experiment to any item—you just have to have enough of them to give one to each girl, and they should be of varied quality and value. (Other ideas might include bracelets, serving dishes, hats, cell phones & iPods, or CDs.)

- **Printouts of any online results from this week's quiz.**

PREPARATION

Makeover Challenge: One of this week's challenge ideas is to have a "stay-at-home party." You could model that idea for your group by having an impromptu party on the spot. The key to this party is to limit yourself to what you already have around the house or meeting room—that means not buying any additional food, not renting any movies, not buying any games or supplies for activities. Just make your fun with what's there! Find more suggestions on the Ideas Bulletin Board online at: www.headtosoulmakeover.com.

 # CHAT ABOUT IT 10 MINUTES

Start off the lesson with the following ice-breaker question to get the group recalling their experience with their Makeover Challenge from last week. Encourage them to use examples from their Makeover Journals to contribute to the discussion.

Did you write anything in your Makeover Journal last week about getting to know someone who would normally irritate you, purposefully ignoring a pet peeve, or pausing before a decision? Share a situation where you exercised more patience than usual.

Here's the show you've been waiting for...you are being featured on *My Super Sweet 16!* This show follows real-life teenagers as they prepare to celebrate their sixteenth birthday with a party where no expense is spared! Here's what you might experience on the show:

NOTE: The parties described here were actually featured on the show. This lesson is perhaps the most directly related to the overall theme of the whole study: *Becoming Real in a Fake World.* This reality show that we are using to consider the topic of envy gives us a glimpse into a world that seems about as fake as it gets. Encourage your group to think about what it means to be real, genuine, and content, and to consider how much more attractive these qualities are in comparison to being superficial, spoiled, boastful, demanding, and ungrateful.

- A Fantasy-Land party, where you make a grand entrance dressed in a showgirl costume and riding on an elephant, with a complete carnival, and a gift of a Range Rover.

- A Diamonds Are Forever party, where you're carried in on the shoulders of two hulking men, and given a 7-carat diamond ring and a $100,000 Mercedes sedan.

- The Fairy Tale party in a castle tent, where you arrive in a Cinderella carriage, have knights as your bodyguards, see a fireworks show in your honor, and receive the gift of a new BMW.

What kind of theme would you want for your ideal Super Sweet 16 party? If you could have the party anywhere in the world, where would you hold it? Who would be your guest performer? What kind of food would you serve? What would you wear?

MY SUPERFICIAL SWEET 16

My Super Sweet 16 is an entertaining—and sometimes sickening—look at the tantrums and meltdowns that some very rich girls have in the process of receiving a party that's lavish beyond imagination. These girls are bent on creating for themselves what could be called the most fake world of all—a world where they get everything they want, and they go to extremes to appear popular. It's all supposed to be super—but usually it just ends up feeling *superficial*. Here are three types of superficiality, as shown in these exact quotes from girls on the show:

- I WANT IT ALL: This is the girl who grasps for every *thing*—from jewels to clothes to cars—and declares, "I'm used to getting everything I want, and if I don't...look out."

- IT'S ALL ABOUT ME: This girl thrives when the world revolves around her: "I love being the center of attention, when everything's focused on me."

- HOW DO I RATE? This girl obsesses about comparing herself to others: "I have to stand out among everyone else, and I have to be the hottest thing at my party."

Each of these girls got what she wanted—the gifts, the attention, the status. So, why weren't they satisfied? Because each of them was trying to find happiness in something superficial.

 ## CHECK YOURSELF 10 MINUTES

Well, you're about to be featured on our Head-to-Soul version of the show. We're calling it _My Superficial Sweet 16_. Right now, you'll find out how content you are as you rate how superficial or super-satisfied you'd feel in various situations.

Take the _My Superficial Sweet 16 Tally_ now or online at www.headtosoulmakeover.com.

Read the instructions aloud. This is a simple multiple-choice test. The scenarios are intended to help the girls think of how they might react in various situations. Encourage them not to take the possible reactions too literally. If they read the choices and say, "I wouldn't do any of these," encourage them to adjust the wording to make one of the choices fit, or to think more generally and choose the one that most resembles how they would react.

Take the self-assessment yourself, making mental adjustments to the situations for your own context, and be willing to share your results.

My Superficial SWEET 16
TALLY

Do you look for happiness in superficial things like possessions, attention, or status? Find out just how superficial or super-satisfied you are by selecting how you'd be most likely to respond in each situation.

1. Your friend just got a new iPhone, and you don't have one. How do you respond when she's showing it off?

    a. I wish I could convince my parents to get me an iPhone.

    b. I change the subject and tell about something new I got recently.

    c. I think about some way in which I am luckier than her, and that makes me feel better.

    d. I'm happy for her and I ask to see how the phone works.

2. You are working on a group project. How do you act?

    a. I'll do whatever it takes to get a good grade, and I'll make sure I get the grade I deserve even if other group members flake out.

    b. I want to be in charge of the group, because it seems like my ideas are better than other people's.

    c. I find myself evaluating who is doing how much work to make sure everything's fair.

    d. I contribute my best work for the good of the group, and I try to be affirming and encouraging of other group members along the way.

3. You need a new pair of jeans. What is your shopping tactic?

    a. I look for a name brand that will impress my friends.

    b. I take my friends with me and buy the jeans they say look best on me.

    c. I look at what the hot girls are wearing and try to buy that.

    d. I buy the jeans that I feel best in and that I can afford.

4. You are having friends over. You know their houses are bigger than yours. How do you feel about your house?

   a. I am embarrassed because I don't think my house is good enough.

   b. I just wish my parents would give me a private area where my friends and I could hang out and have fun.

   c. I think about a friend's house and wish my house was like hers.

   d. Even though my house isn't perfect, I enjoy sharing it with my friends.

5. Your friend is talking about the dinner her family had together. Your family hasn't eaten together since Christmas. How does her talk make you feel?

   a. I can't relate. My family isn't like that—and I wish it was.

   b. I'm depressed. I say my family never has dinner together, and I hope people notice how sad I am.

   c. I think she's so lucky. Everything about her family sounds so perfect, and I imagine they always get along.

   d. I'm interested in her experience, and I ask questions about how the dinner went.

6. A group of your friends decide to go to a concert, but you're not allowed to go because it's on a school night. How do you react?

   a. I have a meltdown because this was a once-in-a-lifetime opportunity, and I mope around for the rest of the night.

   b. I complain to my friends about my strict parents and hope to get a little sympathy.

   c. I feel jealous and wish I had cool parents like everyone else. It's unfair that they got to go and I didn't.

   d. Although I was disappointed I couldn't go, I enjoy looking at my friends' pictures and hearing about their fun evening.

7. You are at the Homecoming game. Which of these activities are you most likely to do?

   a. I look at the football players and daydream about going out with one of them.

   b. I envy the homecoming queen because she's the center of attention and seems so popular.

   c. I gossip about the cheerleaders and check out who's sitting with who.

   d. I enjoy the game and have fun with my friends.

8. You are having lunch at school. Which of these things happens most often?

   a. I eye my friend's cute outfit and think about what I need to go out and buy.

   b. I pull out my mirror to check how I look.

   c. I envy the couples around me.

   d. I eat my lunch and enjoy my friends.

9. A popular girl walks by. What goes through your mind?

   a. I check out what she's wearing and wish I could shop where she does.

   b. I think about how many friends she has and how happy she must be, and I wish I could trade places with her.

   c. I find something to criticize about her.

   d. I admire her, and something about her makes me just say a quick prayer for her.

10. It's Friday night, and you have nothing to do. What do you tell yourself about that?

    a. I can't sit still. I have to come up with something to do or I'll go crazy.

    b. How humiliating. How could I have a Friday night by myself? Everyone has forgotten about me, and they don't care that I'm all alone!

c. What's wrong with me? I'm sure they're all out together and they left me out on purpose.

d. I love having an evening to myself to kick back and relax!

SO...ARE YOU SUPERFICIAL OR SUPER-SATISFIED?

Add up all your A's, B's, C's and D's to find the answer!

OOPS! I'M SUPERFICIAL!

Total A's_____ **I Want It All!** I am most likely to be discontent with what I have and think I'll be happy if I get more things.

Total B's_____ **It's All About Me!** I am most likely to think I'd be happier if I were more popular.

Total C's_____ **How Do I Rate?** I am most likely to compare myself with other people and think I'd be happier if I were like them or better than them.

GUESS WHAT? I'M SUPER-SATISFIED!

Total D's_____ I am most likely to feel happy a lot of the time because I'm content with who I am and what I have.

When everyone has finished scoring the quiz, ask the following question.

In what areas do you tend to be the most discontent?

TRY IT OUT 10 MINUTES

THE CONTENTMENT EXPERIMENT

Now it's time to distribute the purses (or other items, as explained in the Materials Needed section). As you hand an item to each participant, say to her, "You ARE this purse." When everyone has been given a purse, go around the circle and have everyone answer the following questions (replacing the word "item" with the name of the item you distributed). Quick answers are all that is needed for this exercise.

As a way of illustrating how contentment works, your leader is going to pass out a variety of items to the group. After you receive an item imagine that you *are* the item you've been given. Think about these questions:

What is it about being this item that you are dissatisfied with?

I'm missing a strap; I am too small to fit anything; I don't match any of my outfits; etc.

Look around and choose someone else's item that you would rather be. Why would you choose to be that item?

She's more practical; she has rhinestones; that one's my favorite color; etc.

Shift your thinking now, and list reasons why you are thankful you are this item.

I'm small/large; I have lots of compartments; etc.

What can you learn about contentment from this exercise?

There are so many possible insights, including these: Contentment is all about what you focus on; comparison leads to discontentment; contentment is a choice; you can develop contentment by practicing being thankful; etc.

The rest of the lesson draws upon the girls' experiences in this Contentment Experiment.

TALK IT OVER 20 MINUTES

Transition from the quiz results and the experiment to the lesson. Read the setup of the *Three Ways to Get Super-Satisfied,* which is another way of saying three ways to become content, happy, thankful, genuine, and real. Encourage the girls to think about this: It's entirely possible that if a person becomes all these things, she'd be well-liked by many people—she would be truly popular.

THREE WAYS TO GET SUPER-SATISFIED

There are three kinds of behavior that lead to discontentment: Coveting things, comparing yourself to others, and being jealous of attention. If you want to become real in a fake world, you will work on replacing these types of discontentment with super-satisfaction. Then you will be a genuine person—and more likeable too!

1. CHOOSE CONTENTMENT OVER COVETING

In our Contentment Experiment we started by complaining about things we were dissatisfied with. It can become a habit to look at our circumstances and always wish things were different.

There's a famous story that describes exactly what can happen when we covet (long for or crave) what we don't have. It's one of Aesop's Fables—maybe you even read it as a child. In the story of "The Dog and the Shadow," a dog walks across a bridge, carrying a piece of meat in his mouth. Looking down he sees his own reflection in the water. He thinks, "That dog has a mighty fine-looking piece of meat, and I want it!" So the dog snaps at the shadow in the water— but when he opens his mouth, the piece of meat he had drops into the water and is lost. The moral of the story is: *If you covet all, you may lose all.*

What kinds of things do you find yourself wishing for? When have you become so preoccupied with what you don't have that you stop enjoying what you do have?

The Bible describes what happens when you love things too much.

> *But godliness with contentment is great gain. For we brought nothing into the world, and we can take nothing out of it. But if we have food and clothing, we will be content with that. Those who want to get rich fall into temptation and a trap and into many foolish harmful desires that plunge people into ruin and destruction. For the love of money is a root of all kinds of evil.* **(1 Timothy 6:6-10)**

Imagine that you must choose between a million dollars and contentment. Which would you choose—and why?

Help the group come to the conclusion that contentment is more important than money. Without contentment you'll never be happy, no matter how much money you have. But with contentment, you can be happy in any circumstance. Contentment is a very powerful character quality!

What does this passage say is a "trap"? How do we avoid that trap?

Wanting to get rich is a trap. We get out of the trap by combining godliness with contentment—seeking to be more like God, and more thankful to God.

2. STOP COMPARING AND START REJOICING

The next part of our Contentment Experiment was to compare your item with someone else's, and think about why you'd rather have the other item. Another word for that desire for what someone else has is envy, and *envy* starts with comparison. Whenever you find you're comparing yourself to someone else, watch out! You're headed for one of two problems. If you compare and say, "I didn't get what she got—that's not fair!" then you can easily get *jealous*. If you compare and say, "She doesn't have what I have—sure glad I'm not her." then you get *prideful*. How do you stop comparing? Try to follow this advice:

Rejoice with those who rejoice, and weep with those
who weep. **(Romans 12:15, NASB)**

Which part of this verse is harder for you—to be happy with others when they are happy, or to be sad with them when they are sad? How does rejoicing with those who rejoice cure jealousy? How can it cure pride?

This scriptural concept of "rejoicing with those who rejoice" can be a difficult one for teenagers (and adults) to apply in real life. Think of the kid who whines "that's not fair" whenever a sibling gets a treat. It should be easy for the girls to come up with situations when they've had a hard time rejoicing for someone else who got special treatment.

Rejoicing with those who rejoice doesn't always cure jealousy, but it is stronger than jealousy. Rejoicing for others can't coexist with jealousy. Rejoicing with those who rejoice takes the focus off ourselves and helps increase the happiness of others by adding our rejoicing to theirs. Jealousy happens when we compare ourselves to someone else. But, in order to rejoice with those who rejoice, we have to be purely thinking about others and not about ourselves. The minute we start comparing, we open ourselves to jealousy, and we can't rejoice for them!

Rejoicing with those who rejoice also overcomes certain types of pride. It's impossible to indulge in the pride of entitlement ("I deserve special treatment," or "the world revolves around me") and rejoice with those who rejoice at the same time. We can't genuinely celebrate someone else's good fortune if we're feeling pridefully superior ("Even though she got a new outfit, my clothes are better than hers").

3. IT'S NOT ALL ABOUT ME...IT'S ALL ABOUT YOU!

This section discusses Joseph's status in his family, and how jealous his brothers were of Joseph's being the favored son.

Joseph's brothers had a problem. Ever since their baby brother Joseph was born, he was their father's favorite. He got all the attention, he never did anything wrong, and he even got a special gift from Dad that no one else received—a coat of many colors. His brothers were so jealous, they got rid of Joseph by selling him into slavery. (See Genesis 37 for the rest of Joseph's exciting story.)

Have you ever envied someone who was the center of attention? Do you ever do things in order to become the center of attention, to be more popular, or to be loved?

If we were able to talk to Joseph's brothers, they might tell us they just wanted to feel special. They wanted their father's attention and approval, so they tried to get rid of anyone who was in their way. Instead of thinking about their youngest brother's well-being, or about how losing him would break their father's heart, they thought only of themselves. They said, "It's all about me." The cure for "It's all about me" is to turn it into "It's all about you." How? 1 Corinthians 13:4 tells us love is not jealous—it does not envy. In fact, love cancels out envy. Envy is all about *me*; love is all about *you*.

If Joseph's brothers had chosen to love Joseph instead of envying him, what might have happened between them and their father? Are there any situations in your family or at school in which loving others would work better for you than trying to make sure you are loved?

CHECK IN WITH YOUR MAKEOVER TEAM
10 MINUTES

Read the following instructions for the Makeover Teams to reinforce what they should be doing together during their team time. Then, from the Makeover Journal section, read through the Makeover Challenge options and provide clarification as needed.

The Makeover Bonus Challenge would be a particularly helpful one to get your whole group to try together. Enhance it by making it a competition to see who can say more than 16 thank yous per day. It is important that the girls develop the practice of writing down what they're thankful for—it's a great visual reminder of how blessed they are.

Have the group split into teams for their accountability discussion. After the teams have had their discussions and prayed together, bring the entire group back together and close the meeting in prayer. If you want them to do next week's quiz ahead of time, remind them now.

Based on your assessment results, share with your team how superficial or super-satisfied you are. Go to your Makeover Journal for this week and choose your Makeover Challenge; share with your team which one you chose and why. Pray for one another about the areas where each of you needs to develop more contentment. Set up a time and a way to connect during the week to encourage one another and to read aloud at least one day's "16 Thank Yous." If you haven't been connecting during the week, figure out why, and make it happen this week!

MAKEOVER JOURNAL WEEK 7

CHOOSE A MAKEOVER CHALLENGE

Transform yourself into a super-satisfied person by choosing the Makeover Challenge that helps you be more content in the area in which you struggle. Keep track of your progress toward "becoming real in a fake world" in your Makeover Journal or online blog.

If you scored highest in...	...try this Makeover Challenge to become more content.
I Want It All	☐ **Have a "Stay at Home" Party.** Instead of going out, go through your house and find books you haven't read, games you haven't played, crafts you haven't done, or foods you've never tried. Try them out—and enjoy what you already have.
It's All About Me	☐ **Change Your Focus.** Seek to listen to others, let them have the spotlight, and quietly pray for them instead of jumping in and telling your story.
How Do I Rate?	☐ **Say "No" to Envy.** Do your best to "rejoice with those who rejoice" and genuinely show happiness for others when good things happen in their lives.

MAKEOVER BONUS CHALLENGE: 16 THANK YOUS

One great way to develop contentment is to work on being thankful for what you have already. Compete with yourself every day this week to try to say "thank you" for 16 different things per day. Give yourself one point for every time you thank God for something, and for every time you thank a person for anything throughout the day. (It might be your parent, a restaurant server, a teacher, your friend.) Keep score by making brief notes in your Makeover Journal, or by trying the online Thank-You Counter at www.headtosoulmakeover.com. If your whole group has at least five days of 16 Thank Yous this week, reward yourselves!

DATE: _____

Today, I became super-satisfied by being content when…

_____

_____

16 Thank Yous (*List the things for which you said thank you*)

1 _____	2 _____	3 _____	4 _____
5 _____	6 _____	7 _____	8 _____
9 _____	10 _____	11 _____	12 _____
13 _____	14 _____	15 _____	16 _____

DATE: _____

Today, I became super-satisfied by being content when…

_____

_____

16 Thank Yous (*List the things for which you said thank you*)

1 _____	2 _____	3 _____	4 _____
5 _____	6 _____	7 _____	8 _____
9 _____	10 _____	11 _____	12 _____
13 _____	14 _____	15 _____	16 _____

DATE: _____

Today, I became super-satisfied by being content when…

_____

_____

16 Thank Yous (List the things for which you said thank you)

1 _____ 2 _____ 3 _____ 4 _____
5 _____ 6 _____ 7 _____ 8 _____
9 _____ 10 _____ 11 _____ 12 _____
13 _____ 14 _____ 15 _____ 16 _____

DATE: _____

Today, I became super-satisfied by being content when…

_____

_____

16 Thank Yous (List the things for which you said thank you)

1 _____ 2 _____ 3 _____ 4 _____
5 _____ 6 _____ 7 _____ 8 _____
9 _____ 10 _____ 11 _____ 12 _____
13 _____ 14 _____ 15 _____ 16 _____

DATE: _____

Today, I became super-satisfied by being content when…

_____

_____

16 Thank Yous (List the things for which you said thank you)

1 _____ 2 _____ 3 _____ 4 _____
5 _____ 6 _____ 7 _____ 8 _____
9 _____ 10 _____ 11 _____ 12 _____
13 _____ 14 _____ 15 _____ 16 _____

DATE: _____

Today, I became super-satisfied by being content when…

_____

_____

16 Thank Yous *(List the things for which you said thank you)*

1 _____ 2 _____ 3 _____ 4 _____

5 _____ 6 _____ 7 _____ 8 _____

9 _____ 10 _____ 11 _____ 12 _____

13 _____ 14 _____ 15 _____ 16 _____

DATE: _____

Today, I became super-satisfied by being content when…

_____

_____

16 Thank Yous *(List the things for which you said thank you)*

1 _____ 2 _____ 3 _____ 4 _____

5 _____ 6 _____ 7 _____ 8 _____

9 _____ 10 _____ 11 _____ 12 _____

13 _____ 14 _____ 15 _____ 16 _____

EPISODE 8

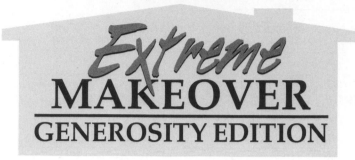

This lesson is based on the reality show, *Extreme Makeover: Home Edition*. To learn more about the show or watch episodes, go to the Web site: http://abc.go.com/primetime/xtremehome/.

SHOW SYNOPSIS

Extreme Makeover: Home Edition is a reality television series in which a family's house, including all rooms, exterior, and landscaping, is made over by a team of builders and designers in seven days while the family, who is in need of new hope because of an illness, a death in the family, or a disaster that has left them destitute, goes off on vacation.

A local home builder and community volunteers build the structure while the design team works on the creative aspects of the house, incorporating the family's interests as design inspiration. Show host, Ty Pennington, selects a portion of the house to be his "Secret Room," which no one can view prior to the final reveal.

At the end of the week, the family returns to their home, to see cheering crowds and the view of their home blocked by a bus. When Ty and the family give the order, "Bus driver, move that bus!!" the family sees the end result of the team's efforts. Ty's "secret room" is often a child's bedroom (often for a special-needs youth), the parents' master bedroom, or a home-based business. Some episodes feature special gifts given to the family by outside parties, such as mortgage pay-offs, college scholarships, or automobiles.

MATERIALS NEEDED

- **16 Thank Yous Reward:** Have a small reward to give girls who achieved the goal of saying thank you 16 times a day for at least five days last week. Since this contest was a reinforcement of the lesson on Contentment, you could go beyond the trinket-type reward and give the reward of a one-time gift made in the name of your group to a worthy cause, such as the support of a child through Compassion International (a set sum of money for every girl who achieved the goal). You might also consider rewarding them with some kind of group outing that would further the emphasis on contentment (and generosity), such as a work day at a women's shelter.

- **Makeover Generosity-Style:** One set of the following supplies to use with each makeover recipient

  - Curling iron

  - Hairbrush and/or comb

  - Hair ties or clasps, bobby pins, hairbands

  - Hairspray

  - Makeup (foundation, blush, eye shadow, eye liner, lip gloss. Avoid mascara unless it's new)

  - Nail files

  - Nail polish (maybe a couple of bottles since 4 people will be painting nails)

- Printouts of any online results from this week's quiz.

 # CHAT ABOUT IT 10 MINUTES

Start off the lesson by seeing how everyone did on the 16 Thank Yous Bonus Challenge. Give small prizes to the girls who achieved the goal. Consider giving a group reward or planning a celebration that reinforces the concept of Contentment (see reward ideas above).

Ask the following ice-breaker question to get the group recalling their experience with their Makeover Challenge from last week. Encourage them to refer to examples from their Makeover Journals to contribute to the discussion.

Let's start off by seeing how everyone did on the 16 Thank Yous Bonus Challenge. Share something about your experience of trying to be more thankful—how did it affect you? Did you find yourself feeling more content? Compare the number of thank yous that each of you said—and celebrate!

Now, look over the Makeover Challenge section of your journal and share how you practiced being more content this past week. Did you have a "stay at home" party and enjoy things you already have? Did you focus on others and resist telling your own story? Did you rejoice with those who were rejoicing?

The following ice-breaker question will help the girls realize that generosity goes beyond giving money. Each person on the *Extreme Makeover* team gives his or her skills and talents. As various girls talk about which member of the team they'd enjoy being, help them think about the skills and talents they have that they can give away generously.

This week you get to be part of the team on *Extreme Makeover: Home Edition*. This show finds a family that's going through a difficult time, and builds them a new house that will help give them a fresh start.

Which of the following members of the *Extreme Makeover* team would you most enjoy being and why?

- **The Team Leader (Ty):** He inspires the team and volunteers to meet big goals, and shows his own artistic flair by working the entire week by himself on a secret room for one family member.

- **The Carpenter (Paige):** In her pink hardhat and pink toolbelt, she has the carpentry skills to build beautiful kitchen cabinets and specialty furniture for children's rooms.

- **The Designer (Paul):** He has an amazing imagination, and his job is to design extravagantly themed rooms around each family member's hobbies.

- **The Shopper (Tracy):** Her role on the team is to go shopping! She acquires all the furniture and decor, and the useable items that fill the cupboards, closets, drawers, and walls.

LET'S DO IT!

After the *Extreme Makeover* team decides to take on a new project, they huddle, stack hands, and call out, "Let's do it!!!" And, wow, do they do it! It takes different types of generosity to get the job done:

- *Generosity with Talents:* We see all kinds of gifted people on the show, donating what they do best—decorating, hammering, planting, painting, organizing, even doing a musical performance.

- *Generosity with Time:* Hundreds of volunteers show up to help build a house in seven days. The people on the show are generous with their time, often working throughout the night to finish the job on time.

- *Generosity with Things:* Whenever you see the family given a special surprise gift—such as a new car, money to pay off a mortgage, or prepaid college education for the children—you know that behind it are generous people who are good at giving away their money and their things.

 ## CHECK YOURSELF 10 MINUTES

On our *Extreme Makeover: Generosity Edition* show, you get to see which kind of generosity you do best. Are you most generous with your things, your talents, or your time?

Take the *Extreme Makeover: Generosity Edition Survey.*

Read the instructions aloud. This is a multiple-choice test with a twist— the letters for the answers stand for secret words that are not revealed until the scoring. If the girls have trouble selecting an answer because none of them seem to fit, encourage them to interpret the answers more generally and adjust the wording as necessary to help find responses that fit them.

Take the self-assessment yourself, making mental adjustments to the situations for your own context, and be willing to share your results.

SURVEY

Do you use your things, your talents, and your time to help others—or only for your own good? If you are more "all about yourself" than about giving to others, then your generosity might need an Extreme Makeover. Circle the letter corresponding with your most honest answer to each question.

1. How do you respond to interruptions (phone calls, mom asking you to do something, sibling wanting something)?

   V   I try to set aside what I'm doing and meet the person's need.

   T   I usually feel impatient, because they are interfering with my agenda.

   D   If the interruption is important, I set aside what I'm doing.

2. If a friend wants to borrow your favorite sweater, how do you feel?

   S   As a rule I don't lend out my clothes or my stuff.

   G   What's mine is yours! Enjoy using it!

   P   I let her borrow it, but I feel nervous about it. I don't want it to be ruined or lost.

3. The new girl wants to join your group for lunch. How do you feel?

   C   Awkward! What is she thinking? Our group is just too well-established, and she'll feel out of place.

   M   I don't mind if she sits with us, but I wouldn't go out of my way to strike up a conversation with her. I usually let my more outgoing friends do that.

   H   I'd welcome her, help her get to know everyone, and ask her about herself to try to help her feel comfortable.

4. When someone desperately asks for help with something you don't enjoy doing (cleaning up after an event, doing yardwork, taking care of kids, helping a friend study, etc.), what's your answer?

D I'm not sure. Depends on what else I have to do.

V I can always find time to help!

T My schedule is too full.

5. When you hear about a tragedy (someone's house burned down, a starving orphan in Africa, flood victims), how do you respond?

P I might see if my parents will send a check to help.

G I try to figure out a way to raise money to help (go without something for a week, donate my allowance, organize a fundraising drive, etc.).

S I feel sorry for them, but that's as far as it goes.

6. What do you do with your hobby?

M My hobby gets me recognition (I perform; I enter contests; I make things to give to friends).

C My hobby is mostly for my own enjoyment (I play my guitar in my room; I collect movie star memorabilia).

H I use my hobby to help others (I make things to give away to needy people; I perform for groups to encourage them; I use my talent to help people).

7. What do you do at church?

T I go to church now and then.

D I go to church and youth services on a regular basis.

V I do things for my personal spiritual growth, and I volunteer regularly (teach children, clean the building, lead worship, welcome visitors, work in the nursery, etc.).

8. The kid next to you in class keeps asking you for help. What do you feel?

    C   Irritation, like, "Your stupidity is not my problem. Ask someone who cares!"

    H   I try to help if it's appropriate. I like helping people.

    M   Tolerance, like, "I'll help you this one time, but I wish you'd figure it out yourself."

9. How often do you volunteer in the community (visit a seniors' residence, feed homeless people, help in a kids' club, etc.)?

    T   I have never really done that. I don't have time, or I don't know how to get involved.

    V   At least once a month.

    D   Once or twice a year.

10. What do you do with your money?

    P   I use my money for entertainment and gas and clothes, and once in a while I give something in the church offering.

    S   I only have enough money for my basic needs, so it all goes for that.

    G   I give a percentage of my money to church or charity regularly, and the rest I save or spend.

11. Your mom asks if you'd be willing to babysit three kids on Saturday so your neighbor (a single mom) can get away for the day. What is your first thought?

    H   How cool that there is something I can do to help!

    C   Will she pay me?

    M   What if I don't like her kids? Then it won't be any fun.

12. If you have two homemade cookies in your lunch, what do you do?

    G   I automatically offer the second one to the person I'm sitting with.

    S   I try to eat them in private so no one else will see them and ask for one.

    P   If someone asks me for one, I'll give it away...reluctantly.

DOES YOUR GENEROSITY NEED AN EXTREME MAKEOVER?

Count each letter and see how generous you are. Scores of 3 or 4 are a strong trend.

Are you generous with your THINGS and money?

Total S's_____   **Stingy:** I hoard my things and don't like sharing.

Total P's_____   **Possessive:** I share when I have to, but you might have to pry my fingers loose.

Total G's_____   **Generous:** I don't view my things as my own, and I enjoy giving to bless others.

Are you generous with your TALENTS and skills?

Total C's_____   **Closed:** I'm closed to people and not willing to put myself out to meet the needs of others.

Total M's_____   **Me-centered:** If it's good for me, then I'll help.

Total H's_____   **Helpful:** I use my abilities for the good of others.

Are you generous with your TIME and agenda?

Total T's_____   **Time Hoarder:** My time is too precious to let other people infringe on my schedule.

Total D's_____   **Drifter:** My schedule fills up with whatever seems important or meets my needs that particular day.

Total V's_____   **Volunteer:** I purposefully give some of my time away on a regular basis.

When everyone has finished scoring the quiz, ask the following question.

Take a look at the areas where you scored 3 or 4 points. Do you see a strong generous trend (high G, H, or V), or do you have a stronger trend toward holding things for yourself (high S, C, or T)?

Some girls may find that this quiz doesn't point to any strong trends, because there are only four questions per category. If the quiz itself doesn't reveal a clear answer, have the participants read through the score key and assess for themselves where they feel they are the strongest or weakest.

TRY IT OUT   10 MINUTES

GIVE A MAKEOVER...GENEROSITY-STYLE

Choose one group member to be the recipient of a generosity-style makeover, where all the other group members contribute in various ways to her makeover.

Choose the recipient randomly, or maybe even in a way that might seem unfair (the girl with the same hair color as you, the one who chose "S" as the answer to Question 12, the one who wore green shoes—something that might trigger a twinge of jealousy in the other girls!). If you have more than 7 girls in your group, split into groups of 5-7, and choose one girl to be the makeover recipient for each group.

Provide the girls with supplies, and have them simultaneously give the recipient a "makeover." Assign each of the following roles to a different girl:

- Hairstylist
- Makeup artist
- Left hand fingernail polish
- Right hand fingernail polish
- Left foot toenail polish
- Right foot toenail polish

Allow only five minutes for the makeover. If they're not done in five minutes, that's great. The frustration they feel at not finishing could become part of their observations about how it feels to show generosity ("It feels so good that I hate to quit").

What kinds of generosity were exhibited?

Generosity with my skills; generosity with my time; generosity with giving something different from money; generosity that helps someone else feel good about herself.

How did it feel to show that kind of generosity?

Go for the deeper reflections here! (I forgot it could feel so good to be a giver. I wish I'd had time to finish. I think I had more fun than the recipient did. I would have rather been a hairstylist than a hair-stylee.)

Recipient: What was it like to receive that kind of generosity?

The recipient may have totally savored the experience, may have felt some pain if her hair got pulled, may have felt frustrated that the makeover wasn't done as she'd have preferred, or may have felt awkward at being the center of attention. Point out that that spectrum of feelings is typical of many who are on the receiving end of another's generosity.

How did you feel about the fact that only one person received a makeover?

Here's a true confessions moment. Did the girls experience envy? A feeling that it wasn't fair? A yearning to have the chance to get a makeover? Relieved that they weren't picked to receive a makeover?

 ## TALK IT OVER   20 MINUTES

Transition from the makeover to the lesson. Read the setup of the *Three Steps to an Extreme Generosity Makeover*.

THREE STEPS TO AN EXTREME GENEROSITY MAKEOVER

If you need to become more generous in some way, follow these three steps to an Extreme Generosity Makeover: Figure out the problem, follow the plan, and feel the pleasure.

STEP 1: FIGURE OUT THE PROBLEM

When the Extreme Makeover team arrives at a family's home, their first job is to figure out what's wrong with the house. In order to start our Generosity Makeover, we need to do the same thing. Match each of the following four Scripture passages with the greed-related problem that can block generosity.

The following chart is a matching exercise that is probably best done together as a group. Have one person read Passage A aloud. Then, the leader slowly reads the four problems aloud, checking with the girls after each one to see if they think it is the match for that Scripture. When they think they have found the match, have them write the problem number in the box next to Passage A. Then have another girl read Passage B. The leader reads through the remaining three problems aloud until the girls find the match for Passage B. Proceed in this fashion to the end of the exercise.

ANSWER KEY:

Passage A: Problem 2   Passage B: Problem 4

Passage C: Problem 3   Passage D: Problem 1

Passage A: 1 Kings 21:2-4 Problem #_____ *Ahab said to Naboth, "Let me have your vineyard to use for a vegetable garden, since it is close to my palace…I will pay you what it is worth." But Naboth replied, "The Lord forbid that I should give you the inheritance of my ancestors." So Ahab went home, sullen and angry…He lay on his bed sulking and refused to eat.*	**Problem 1: PRIDE** It's hard to be generous when you feel so proud of what you worked to gain and really want to hang onto it. But we don't really own our possessions, because even our ability to get what we have was given to us by God.
Passage B: Luke 12:15 Problem #_____ *He [Jesus] said to them, "Watch out! Be on your guard against all kinds of greed; life does not consist in an abundance of his possessions."*	**Problem 2: SELFISHNESS** If you're greedy, your life motto might be, "It's all about me." You shut out everyone else's needs and focus only on your own.
Passage C: Ecclesiastes 5:10 Problem #_____ *Those who love money never have enough; those who love wealth are never satisfied with their income.*	**Problem 3: ANXIETY** A greedy person is characterized by anxiety. When you think you'll only be happy after you have the next thing or achieve the next success, you can never rest.
Passage D: Deuteronomy 8:10-18 Problem #_____ *When you have eaten and are satisfied, praise the Lord your God for the good land he has given you…Otherwise…your heart will become proud and…you may say to yourself, "My power and the strength of my hands have produced this wealth for me." But remember the Lord your God, for it is he who gives you the ability to produce wealth.*	**Problem 4: INSECURITY** If you think your self-worth is improved by what you own, what you wear, what you drive, or where you live, then greed is faking you out. Having more doesn't make you more secure.

Describe why one or more of these problems makes it hard for you to be generous. Try explaining the Scripture that goes with your problem in your own words.

This question opens the whole topic up for a general discussion. You may need to prompt answers by specifically asking, "Does anyone have an issue with being so proud of something you've worked hard for that it's difficult for you to let it go?"

Use this opportunity to get the girls to interpret Scripture for themselves. The exercise of restating in their own words the passages that apply to their situations helps them practice an important skill.

STEP 2: FOLLOW THE PLAN

After the Extreme Makeover team figures out the problem, they make a plan for the new house—and then follow that plan as they build. We have a plan for generosity that we can follow, and we can read about it in the story of the poverty-stricken Macedonians in 2 Corinthians. Take a look at what Paul says about the sacrificial generosity the Macedonians expressed toward the persecuted church in Jerusalem. It's a three-part plan for being generous:

> *They are being tested by many troubles, and they are very poor. But they are also filled with abundant joy, which has overflowed in rich generosity. For I can testify that they gave not only what they could afford, but far more. And they did it of their own free will. They begged us again and again for the privilege of sharing in the gift for the believers in Jerusalem. They even did more than we had hoped, for their first action was to give themselves to the Lord and to us, just as God wanted them to do.* **(2 Corinthians 8:2-5, NLT)**

Part A: Don't be held back by what you lack. *They are being tested by many troubles, and they are very poor. But they are also filled with abundant joy, which has overflowed in rich generosity.* **The Macedonians were tested by great troubles and were very poor. Yet, they gave much because of their great joy!**

How have your troubles, or your feelings that you don't have enough to spare, kept you from being generous with your time, talents, or things?

Part B: Find the need that tugs your heart. *For I can testify that they gave not only what they could afford, but far more. And they did it of their own free will. They begged us again and again for the privilege of sharing in the gift for the believers in Jerusalem.* **The Macedonians gave more than they could afford, even going so far as to beg and plead for the opportunity to share. They weren't just** *faking* **interest—they were passionately concerned about the plight of the persecuted church in Jerusalem.**

What cause or ministry or need do you feel most passionate about? Why?

This generation of students is great at supporting causes and taking actions that make a difference. Use this time to find out what causes the girls get most excited about. There are sure to be some great ideas among them! This could include gathering supplies to help a family whose house burned down, volunteering at the local animal shelter, or supporting a child through Compassion International.

Part C: Money is fine...but give talents and time! *They even did more than we had hoped, for their first action was to give themselves to the Lord and to us, just as God wanted them to do.* **The Macedonians surprised Paul by giving in a way he did not expect: They went beyond money and gave of themselves. Sometimes, generosity can be faked. Giving money or supporting a child in a developing country can look generous, but sometimes it can be just a way of taking care of guilt or looking good, which is prideful. Likewise you may go on a mission trip for the fun of being with friends, with no real desire to serve the local people. Being real in a fake world means being a** *truly* **generous, others-centered person.**

Beyond your money, what do you have that you can give to the Lord and to others? Share some ways you have given your time or your talents to help others. Can you point to any times you have given with a wrong motivation?

Get the girls to think outside the box about what they have that they can give. Do they know how to knit? They can make afghans for AIDS babies in Africa. Are they good dancers? They can teach inner-city children or entertain at a seniors' residence. When they are sharing past things they've done as a mission or a ministry, affirm the ways they have generously given of themselves to help others.

STEP 3: FEEL THE PLEASURE

The "big reveal" at the end of a home makeover is exciting, because you see the joy on the faces of the family as they receive everyone's generosity. That's the cool thing about giving. You don't lose when you give; your joy multiplies!

> *If you give, you will receive. Your gift will return to you in full measure, pressed down, shaken together to make room for more, and running over. (Luke 6:38, NLT)*

Does this Scripture mean that whatever we give, we'll get the same thing back? How does the pleasure of giving compare with the pleasure of buying something for yourself? What does this verse mean to you, and how does it encourage you to be more generous?

This Scripture has been misused to coerce people to give money in expectation of becoming rich. That's not the idea behind the biblical principle of giving. Although you should not give to get (that isn't generous—it's self-serving), this verse tells us that a natural by-product of giving is receiving—receiving much more than we give! Get the girls to think about the kinds of intangible rewards that come when they are generous.

CHECK IN WITH YOUR MAKEOVER TEAM
10 MINUTES

Read the following instructions for the Makeover Teams to reinforce what they should be doing together during their team time. Then, from the Makeover Journal section, read through the Makeover Challenge options and provide clarification as needed. Have the group split into teams for their accountability discussion. After the teams have had their discussion and prayed together, bring the group back together and close the meeting in prayer. If you want them to do next week's quiz ahead of time, remind them now.

Share with your team how you rated on the *Extreme Makeover: Generosity Edition* assessment. Go to your Makeover Journal for this week and choose your Makeover Challenge, then share with your team which one you chose and why. Pray for one another about becoming more generous. Set up a time and a way to connect during the week to encourage one another and see how you're doing at letting go and being generous.

CHOOSE A MAKEOVER CHALLENGE

Try out your Generosity by choosing a Makeover Challenge that addresses the area in which you have the most trouble letting go. Write about how it feels to exercise that type of generosity in your Makeover Journal or online blog.

If it's hard being generous with your...	...try this Makeover Challenge to develop your generosity.
Things	☐ **Donate something.** I will give away things I don't use, OR I will volunteer at a facility that helps those who have less than I do. (Write about how it feels to help.)
Talents	☐ **Transform your hobby.** I will think of a way to use my hobby or talent to help others this week. (Write about how it feels to use your hobby in a new way.)
Time	☐ **Be interruptible.** I will treat interruptions as opportunities to be generous with my time by giving someone my focused attention as I listen to that person. (Write about how it feels to give up some of your time intentionally.)

DATE: _____

Today, I got a generosity makeover when…

_____

_____

DATE: _____

Today, I got a generosity makeover when…

_____

_____

DATE: _____

Today, I got a generosity makeover when…

_____

_____

DATE: _____

Today, I got a generosity makeover when…

_____

_____

DATE: _____

Today, I got a generosity makeover when…

_____

_____

DATE: _____

Today, I got a generosity makeover when…

_____

_____

DATE: _____

Today, I got a generosity makeover when…

_____

_____

EPISODE 9

THE *REALLY* AMAZING
R A C E

This lesson is based on the reality show, *The Amazing Race*. To learn more about the show or watch episodes, go to the Web site: http://alpha.cbs.com/primetime/amazing_race12/.

SHOW SYNOPSIS

The Amazing Race is a reality game show in which teams literally race around the world. For approximately four weeks, contestants follow clues and use all manner of transportation to reach destinations within multiple countries. During each leg of the race they face a variety of challenges:

1. Detours: The team has to choose between two tasks. One task is typically less physically demanding but is tedious or requires some amount of time or thinking to complete; the other is usually a more physically demanding or frightening option that, depending on the team's ability, may take less time to complete.

2. Roadblocks: Before heading into a Roadblock, teams read a vague clue about the task to come, such as, "Who's *really* hungry?" (for an exotic food-eating challenge), or "Who wants to get down and dirty?" (for a very muddy task). Based only on the clue, they must decide which team member would be best suited to complete the job.

3. Yields: A team can use its "yield" to force another team to stop racing for a period of time. The team using its yield places another team's picture on the YIELD sign. When the yielded team arrives at that station, that team must turn over an hourglass and wait for all the sand to drain before it can continue racing.

Teams are eliminated along the way by coming in last in a leg of the race. The team that finishes the final leg of the journey first is awarded a large cash prize.

MATERIALS NEEDED

- Printouts of any online results from this week's quiz.

 # CHAT ABOUT IT   10 MINUTES

Ask the following ice-breaker question to get the group recalling their experiences with the Makeover Challenge from last week. Encourage them to refer to their Makeover Journals for examples to contribute to the discussion.

Refer to what you wrote in your Makeover Journal last week and share what it felt like to show generosity by donating something, transforming your hobby, or being interruptible.

This week you are competing on *The Amazing Race*. In this contest, teams race around the world, overcoming challenges and problems along the way.

Which of the following actual challenges performed by *Amazing Race* teams would you be most likely to quit, and what is it about it that would make it hard for you to finish?

1. Eating a whole bowl of caviar

2. Carrying a 55-pound side of raw beef a mile

3. Herding 1,000 ducks into a pen 50 yards away

4. Jumping into the hold of a boat and searching for a marked crab among 500 live crabs

5. Walking barefoot on a 220-foot path of jagged stones

6. Taking part in a local seafaring tradition that requires you to have "FF" (for "Fast Forward" challenge) permanently tattooed on your body

THREE REASONS QUITTERS QUIT

For our Head-to-Soul version of *The Amazing Race*, we're calling it *The* Really *Amazing Race*. This is a race that can't be won by a quitter. It definitely takes *perseverance* to overcome the three types of challenges teams encounter during every leg of the race:

- DETOURS are demanding tasks the team must do before moving on. Detours can cause *discouragement*, because you may try and fail, or you fear other people will do better than you.

- A YIELD is something one team can use to force another to stop for a while. Yields are like *criticism*, when people find things wrong with you and make it difficult for you to keep going.

- ROADBLOCKS are challenges that require extra exertion. Roadblocks often cause *frustration* from trying to learn something new, or getting so overwhelmed you lose hope.

 # CHECK YOURSELF

As you compete in *The* Really *Amazing Race*, it's important to discover which type of challenge is most likely to make you quit.

Take the *Quitter's Quiz* now, or online at www.headtosoulmakeover.com.

Read the instructions aloud. This quiz uses the names of the challenges from the reality show as metaphors for the things that can make us want to quit.

Take the self-assessment yourself, making mental adjustments to the situations for your own context, and be willing to share your results.

THE *REALLY* AMAZING RACE

THE QUITTER'S QUIZ

Quitters quit because of discouragement, criticism, or frustration. Think about things you have not finished—examples might include a class, a project, a volunteer job, a relationship, a conversation, a book, a chore, a dream. For each of the following typical reasons to quit, circle your rating:

I.Q. = I Quit
If this happens to a great enough degree, it would probably cause me to quit.

H.I.T. = Hang In There
Even if this happens frequently, I would probably hang in there.

 ## THE DETOUR OF DISCOURAGEMENT

I.Q.	H.I.T.	**BLAME:** I made a stupid mistake, and I'm angry at myself.
I.Q.	H.I.T.	**COMPARISON:** The way I do it isn't as good as the way others do it.
I.Q.	H.I.T.	**MISUNDERSTOOD:** I feel misunderstood and unappreciated.
I.Q.	H.I.T.	**FAILURE:** I tried really hard, but I failed.
I.Q.	H.I.T.	**LAZINESS:** I just don't care anymore.
I.Q.	H.I.T.	**LONELINESS:** I feel all alone, with no one to help me when I need it.
I.Q.	H.I.T.	**LOSS OF INTEREST:** My initial enthusiasm has worn off.
I.Q.	H.I.T.	**OVERCOMMITTED:** I should have never taken this on.
I.Q.	H.I.T.	**POOR HEALTH:** I don't feel well, so I don't have much energy.
I.Q.	H.I.T.	**PROCRASTINATION:** I keep putting it off and avoiding it.
I.Q.	H.I.T.	**STRESSED OUT:** I feel overloaded—just too many things to do.

THE "YIELD" OF CRITICISM

I.Q. **H.I.T.** **CONFLICT:** I argue a lot with others.

I.Q. **H.I.T.** **DIFFICULT PERSON:** That person is hard to work with.

I.Q. **H.I.T.** **FEAR OF DISAPPOINTMENT:** I'm afraid I'll let someone down—or let myself down.

I.Q. **H.I.T.** **FEAR OF RESPONSIBILITY:** If I take this on and it doesn't work, others will blame me.

I.Q. **H.I.T.** **OTHERS' EXPECTATIONS:** I can't reach someone else's high standards.

I.Q. **H.I.T.** **PERSECUTION:** My beliefs are challenged or belittled.

I.Q. **H.I.T.** **PREJUDICE:** I am the object of discrimination or being pre-judged.

I.Q. **H.I.T.** **PUT DOWNS:** I get criticized no matter how hard I try.

I.Q. **H.I.T.** **REJECTION:** I got turned down by someone.

I.Q. **H.I.T.** **UNFAIR ACCUSATION:** I am being punished unjustly.

I.Q. **H.I.T.** **UNSUPPORTED:** A person who's important to me doesn't believe I can do it.

 THE ROADBLOCK OF FRUSTRATION

I.Q. **H.I.T.** **CONFLICTING PRIORITIES:** Something else seems more important.

I.Q. **H.I.T.** **DIFFICULT LEARNING CURVE:** It's hard to learn this new skill/role/subject.

I.Q. **H.I.T.** **FEELS POINTLESS:** I don't have a clear goal or strong direction.

I.Q. **H.I.T.** **HOPELESSNESS:** The task is overwhelming.

I.Q.   **H.I.T.**   **LACK OF RESOURCES:** I don't have enough money/time/facilities/help.

I.Q.   **H.I.T.**   **LOSING:** I'm competitive, and I don't like not winning.

I.Q.   **H.I.T.**   **OUT OF CONTROL:** I'm not in charge, and they're not doing things the best way.

I.Q.   **H.I.T.**   **PAIN:** I have physical discomfort or pain.

I.Q.   **H.I.T.**   **PREVIOUS SUCCESS:** I did well before, but I may not be able to do it again.

I.Q.   **H.I.T.**   **TOO HARD:** I don't have the skills required for success.

I.Q.   **H.I.T.**   **UNCOOPERATIVENESS:** People aren't doing what they're supposed to.

THE QUITTER'S QUIZ SCORECARD

Add up your totals. The area with the highest "I.Q." is the type of problem that is most likely to make you quit.

	Total I.Q.'s	**Total H.I.T.'s**
Discouragement	_____	_____
Criticism	_____	_____
Frustration	_____	_____
Total ALL "Hang In Theres"	_____	

23-33 H.I.T.'s: Your perseverance makes you "Most likely to finish the race."

12-22 H.I.T.'s: You might complete the race—but only if you don't encounter too many problems.

1-11 H.I.T.'s: You are voted "Most likely to quit, due to circumstances."

When everyone has finished scoring the quiz, ask the following questions.

Some of you share what type of quitter you are, and tell a story about a time you missed out on something because you quit. Why is the quality of perseverance so important in life?

TRY IT OUT 5 MINUTES

If your group exhibits any impatience with this next exercise, this is a perfect teaching moment! "Are you tired of taking tests? This is precisely the time perseverance comes into play. When you're bored with a repetitive task, when something takes a lot of brain power, or when you don't feel like finishing, it takes **perseverance** to end well."

Have the girls work together as a group or in pairs to complete the word search exercise.

HOW TO PERSEVERE

Work together to complete the word search using the word list that relates to perseverance.

Place the remaining letters in the blanks to discover how to persevere.

G	H	R	E	N	N	I	W	C	E		COMPETE
E	T	O	U	P	O	D	E	O	M		COMPLETE
N	T	E	P	M	N	P	T	M	O		END
E	R	E	V	E	S	R	E	P	C		FINISH
O	A	H	R	M	U	I	L	E	R		HOPE
E	I	S	T	A	C	Z	P	T	E		MATURE
I	N	I	M	T	C	E	M	E	V		OVERCOME
R	U	N	E	U	E	T	O	H	O		PERSEVERE
T	S	I	S	R	E	P	C	A	N		PERSIST
Y	O	F	U	E	D	F	A	L	L		PRIZE
											RUN
											SUCCEED
											TRAIN
											WINNER

——— —— ———— ———— ————

———————— ———— .

Word Search answer: "GET UP ONE MORE TIME THAN YOU FALL."

Why is this statement a key to persevering? Have you ever had a time in your life when you did this? Describe what happened.

 ## TALK IT OVER 25 MINUTES

Transition from the perseverance word search exercise to the lesson. Begin by reading the setup of the *Three Keys for Finishers*.

THREE KEYS FOR FINISHERS

Quitting is an epidemic these days. Here's how quitter thinking goes: If you've made a commitment to help with a project but you're invited to something that sounds more fun, *quit*. If you're in a friendship, and you have a misunderstanding, *quit*. If that difficult class might ruin your grade point average, *quit*. If a job is boring, *quit*. If your team is having a losing season, *quit*. But here's the problem: Quitters never win; finishers do. If you want to be real in a fake world, you've got to persevere in the race of life. You've got to run that race all the way to the finish. Nothing real is accomplished— no dream is realized, no races are won—without persevering to the end and finishing.

Shout out some things you have accomplished because you had perseverance.

Get the girls to call out things they have done that took perseverance. You're looking for short answers—sort of a fast-paced brainstorming session. Answers could include things like, "Finishing my history project," "Learning a song on the piano," "Cleaning my room," or "Getting third place in cross country." This list will get the group thinking about specific scenarios in which the following biblical concepts can be applied.

Let's find out from the Bible what it takes to be a finisher.

1. FINISHERS FOCUS ON THE PRIZE.

To maintain the highest level of devotion to both their training and the race itself, winning athletes focus on the prize—whether it's the gold medal, the prestige, the world record, or the residual sponsorships and endorsements! When there is a big prize at stake, a true champion will not wreck her concentration by thinking about past failures (which can be paralyzing) or past victories (which can cause carelessness).

> *Forgetting what is behind and straining toward what is ahead, I press on toward the goal to win the prize for which God has called me heavenward in Christ Jesus.* **(Philippians 3:13-14)**

What is the "prize" in the Christian life? What kinds of things should be taking place in a Christian's life between now and reaching the "prize"? (Think about what we've learned in this study, and then envision what God might want to do with your life.)

These questions are designed to get the girls to understand why perseverance is such a big deal for a Christian. In addition to the prize of heaven, there is the process of getting there, which is called life. The way we live our lives can be meaningful and real, or empty and fake. Becoming more and more real by deepening the Christlike character qualities we have been discussing in this study is the way to make the journey of life the most enriching and rewarding. The development of these qualities may result in the birth of a dream to fulfill, a passion to pursue, or a vision to realize. Have the girls imagine for a moment what dreams, passions, or visions God might want them to pursue in their own lives. It's the achievement of those God-given goals that makes life worth living and heaven worth gaining.

How can thinking about past failures make you feel like quitting? How can thinking about past victories make you feel like quitting? How can the ultimate prize motivate you to keep going even when you're discouraged, criticized, or frustrated?

2. FINISHERS GO THROUGH TRAINING.

When a runner prepares for a race, she lifts weights and eats properly, so that her metabolism, muscles, and body weight are all in tune to give her the greatest stamina and the fastest speed. The training we go through in the Christian life involves getting rid of the entanglements that slow us down.

> *Let us throw off everything that hinders and the sin that so easily entangles. And let us run with perseverance the race marked out for us.* (Hebrews 12:1)

Notice that there are two types of things to throw off—hindrances and sin. Hindrances would be things we looked at in the Quitters Quiz that drag us down, like discouragement, criticism, and frustration. But beyond that, there is also sin that can keep us from running well in the spiritual race of life—in the same way that a smoker would have trouble trying to run in the Olympics. If you have a wrong relationship, a bad habit, some problem you're hiding, or a pattern of disobedience, you are sabotaging yourself and making it hard to race.

What are some of the hindrances or sins that entangle you? How do they keep you from achieving what you really want in life? How can you actually "throw them off"?

3. FINISHERS RACE TO THE END.

Stay diligent to the end of the race. If you are trying to have a daily quiet time, and you miss three days in a row, you might think, "I can't be consistent. I'm going to give up." Or, if you are going through a time in your life when you've felt far away from God, you may say, "It's too late. I've wasted so much of my life; I've blown my chance to be of any use to God now." Well, that's quitter thinking. Just because you failed once, or even several times, that doesn't mean you throw in the towel. When you feel like quitting, don't. Your perseverance will do something inside you:

> *Let perseverance finish its work so that you may be mature and complete, not lacking anything.* (James 1:4)

What happens, according to this verse, when you let perseverance finish its work? Imagine yourself "mature and complete"—what kinds of things will be different about you then, compared to the way you are now?

Participants should have a pretty good framework by now (after nine weeks of this study!) to describe what a mature and complete Christian looks like. Have them draw upon specific character qualities from this study to envision what they will be like as they become more Christlike.

 # CHECK IN WITH YOUR MAKEOVER TEAM
10 MINUTES

Read the following instructions for the Makeover Teams to reinforce what they should be doing together during their team time. Give them ideas about ways to have a Makeover Team celebration together this week. Then, from the Makeover Journal section, read through the Makeover Challenge options and provide clarification as needed. Have the group split into teams for their accountability discussion. After the teams have had their discussions and prayed together, bring the whole group back together and close the meeting in prayer.

From *The Quitter's Quiz*, share with your team the kinds of situations that make you most likely to quit. Go to your Makeover Journal for this week and choose your Makeover Challenge; share with your team which one you chose and why. Since this is your last week of the study, get together for a private party with your Makeover Team, and celebrate persevering through this whole study!

CHOOSE A MAKEOVER CHALLENGE

Stop quitting and quit stopping! Choose the Makeover Challenge corresponding with what usually makes you quit. Write about your results in your Makeover Journal or blog about it at www.headtosoulmakeover.com.

If you are most likely to quit due to…	…try this Makeover Challenge to develop more perseverance.
Discouragement	☐ **Try again.** I will choose an area where I've failed (such as having devotions, a sports team tryout, obeying my parents, a subject in school, or kicking a habit), and I will overcome my discouragement and try again.
Criticism	☐ **Improve the quality.** I will choose one task I've grown lazy about doing (such as cleaning my room, helping with dinner, writing papers, practicing an instrument, keeping up with homework) and I will start doing it better—maybe even doing more than what is expected of me.
Frustration	☐ **Finish a project.** I will choose one unfinished project I have been avoiding because it's too big or too hard, and I will tackle it and complete it.

DATE: _____

Today, I showed perseverance when…

_____

_____

DATE: _____

Today, I showed perseverance when…

_____

_____

DATE: _____

Today, I showed perseverance when…

_____

_____

DATE: _____

Today, I showed perseverance when…

_____

_____

DATE: _____

Today, I showed perseverance when…

_____

_____

DATE: _____

Today, I showed perseverance when…

_____

_____

DATE: _____

Today, I showed perseverance when…

_____

_____

EPISODE 10
THE BIG REVEAL PARTY

 ## PARTY PLAN

Schedule the party at a time when you can have at least two or three hours together. If you have more than eight girls in your group, there are suggested adjustments to help you complete everything in the time you have.

MATERIALS NEEDED GENERAL CHECKLIST

- Character foods
- Small prizes and grand prizes for Memory Verse Challenge
- Copies of all party-game handouts
- A pen/pencil for each person
- Small gifts for the Affirmation game

WELCOME ACTIVITY: SELF-PORTRAIT COOKIES
30 MINUTES

Welcome the girls to a cookie-decorating activity as they arrive. Have a selection of cookie decorations laid out, along with snack foods and drinks, and invite each of the girls to decorate a gingerbread girl cookie as a self-portrait of how she looks, now that she has completed her Head-to-Soul Makeover.

Visit the Idea Bulletin Board at www.headtosoulmakeover.com to see what other groups have done in the Big Reveal Party.

What the girls don't know is that *some* of the foods have significance—each of the eight character qualities we have studied is represented by one of the cookie decorating items or snack foods. Let them get started with the decorating and then, midway through, give them this hint:

"While you're making your self-portrait gingerbread girl, we're going to try a little contest. Every one of the eight character qualities we have been studying is represented by at least one of the foods here. Not all of the foods mean something, but some of them do. I'm not going to give you a list of the character qualities—that's part of the game. You have to see if you can remember all eight qualities, and figure out which food stands for each one."

A correct guess identifies the character quality food item—and explains why that item stands for that character quality. There is no prize for this contest.

MATERIALS NEEDED

These materials can be adjusted according to what you can find at your grocery store.

- Camera to take pictures!
- Plain gingerbread girl cookies to decorate (or gingerbread boys, or cupcakes)

CHARACTER QUALITY COOKIE DECORATIONS:

Include additional cookie decorations beyond those on this list, such as M&Ms, licorice strings, peppermints, and chocolate chips. But make sure to include some items that are metaphors for the following character qualities.

- **Confidence:** Nerds candies (even if you feel like a nerd, you can be confident)
- **Contentment:** Green jelly beans (because you shouldn't be green with envy)
- **Perseverance:** Frosting (because frosting "sticks to it")

CHARACTER QUALITY SNACKS TO EAT WHILE DECORATING:

- **Humility:** Cheetos Puffs (because you shouldn't be puffed up with pride)

- **Courage:** Fiery Habañero Doritos (because it takes courage to eat them)

- **Patience:** Tootsie Pops (it requires patience to wait to get to the Tootsie Roll in the middle—without biting)

CHARACTER QUALITY DRINKS:

- **Generosity:** Milk (because cows give their milk—plus, just as giving multiplies your blessings instead of depleting them, the cows' generosity generates more milk)

- **Self-control:** Diet Caffeine-Free Coke and Hawaiian Punch (controlling your sugar & caffeine intake, and controlling your urge to punch someone!)

Take pictures of the girls with their completed self-portrait cookies—before they start eating them!

Then, move to chairs for your discussion time.

 # CHAT ABOUT IT 5 MINUTES

Have your final *Chat About It* time to review last week's lesson.

TIME ALERT: If you've gone overtime on cookie decorating, or if you have more than eight girls in your group, you may want to skip this discussion question about last week's challenge and move right into the setup for the Big Reveal party.

Looking back at last week's Makeover Challenge, share a way you tried again to accomplish a task you'd previously failed, an area where you improved the quality of your work, or a project that you were able to finally finish. How did it feel to persevere?

 **TRY IT OUT**

LET'S HAVE A BIG REVEAL PARTY!

Read the following setup for your Big Reveal party.

Many makeover reality shows end with a Big Reveal party, where friends and family gather to see the results of all the hard work that's been done. Whether it's a room or a whole house or a hairstyle or a wardrobe, the transformation from a makeover is often stunning.

Today we're going to celebrate *your* transformation. It may not feel like you're a totally new person yet. You may feel like you've still got some work to do. Actually, the Bible tells us that there will *always* be work to do, and we won't be finished until we reach heaven. But look what it says about *who* is doing the work:

> *And I am sure that God who began the good work within you will keep right on helping you grow in his grace until his task within you is finally finished on that day when Jesus Christ returns.* (Philippians 1:6, TLB)

This Big Reveal Party is a celebration of the work that has already begun in you—the work that God has begun in you! You have partnered with God and taken some first steps, practiced new skills, thought about Bible truths, and tracked your progress in your journal. Now, it's time to celebrate the good work you have started through this study.

Enjoy the party!

P.S. Go to the online Big Reveal Party at www.headtosoulover.com and sign the Real Girl Wall to commemorate your transformation.

Move into the party activities by reading the following explanation:

"Instead of taking a self-assessment this week, we're going to play some party games! Before I hand out the first game, I'm going to read you the instructions."

MAKEOVER MATCHING GAME INSTRUCTIONS:

Draw lines to match each reality show with the character quality it illustrated. Whoever finishes first with all answers correct wins. Keep your papers face down until everyone has received a copy. When I say, "Go," turn over your paper and begin. Good luck!

MAKEOVER MATCHING GAME 5 MINUTES

MATERIALS NEEDED

- A copy of the "Makeover Matching Game" handout for each participant
- A pen/pencil for each participant

Leader's Hint: There is a non-character quality answer for the first show, which was the overview of all the character qualities. You don't need to mention that ahead of time!

Answer Key:

Total Loser	Self-Control
Fear or Faith Factor	Courage
The Really Amazing Race	Perseverance
Extreme Makeover	Generosity
LifeSwap	Patience
What Not to Be	Head-to-Soul Makeover
My Superficial Sweet 16	Contentment
Don't Replay the Lyrics	Confidence
Prideful Idol	Humility

The winner gets to decide if she'll go first or last in the next game.

MY TOP THREE "WHAT NOT TO BE'S" 15 MINUTES

Read the instructions on the handout aloud, including the two questions. Give the girls time to circle their answers, then have each girl share her top three and answer the two questions. Allow the winner of the Makeover Matching Game to decide whether she'll go first or last.

MATERIALS NEEDED

- A copy of the "My Top Three 'What Not to Be's'" handout for each participant

TIME ALERT: If you have more than eight girls, you can save time by asking each girl to answer only question 2 and to give just one example of something she learned that helped her with one of her character flaws.

MY BEST FEATURE 15 MINUTES

Read the instructions on the handout aloud, including the two questions. Give the girls time to circle their answers, then have each girl answer the two questions.

MATERIALS NEEDED

- A copy of the "My Best Feature" handout for each participant

Leader's Hint: This activity gives the girls a chance to speak positively about themselves to a group, which reinforces the healthy self-talk we learned in connection with the character quality of Confidence. You might want to take notes on what each girl thinks her best feature is in case you want to refer to that later when you're affirming her during the "I Affirm You" activity.

TIME ALERT: If you have more than eight girls, either split into smaller groups or skip this activity.

I AFFIRM YOU 5 MINUTES PER PARTICIPANT

Distribute sets of handouts. Read the instructions aloud. Choose the first girl to be affirmed. That girl waits while everyone else writes a unique affirmation of her. Each member of the group reads her affirmation, and you read yours last. Hand all the "I Affirm You" sheets to the girl, and you give her a small token gift. Proceed to the next girl and repeat the process.

MATERIALS NEEDED

- One set of the "I Affirm You" handouts for each participant. Each girl will be filling out a copy of the handout for every other member of the group. (In a group of eight girls, a set of seven handouts is needed for each girl.) Have the handouts counted out ahead of time to save distribution time.

- A small token gift representing the study to be given to each girl. Gift possibilities might include a car air freshener representing their fragrance in Christ, a small purse mirror which recalls the "He must increase, and I must decrease" lesson, or something that symbolizes becoming real in a fake world (a Pinocchio toy?).

Leader's Hint: You might want to have your own affirmations written out ahead of time. It can be hard to think on the spot, especially when trying to keep the group on task. You read your affirmation last, and give your gift with an explanation: "This represents your fragrance in Christ" then read 2 Corinthians 2:15, or "This is to remind you that he must increase" then read John 3:30, or "Congratulations on being more real in a fake world."

TIME ALERT: Don't wait for everyone to finish writing before you have girls start reading their affirmations. If you have a large group, you might choose to have only five or six people to read their affirmations each time. This is the key exercise of the whole week, but be aware that it can take longer than you expect, so allow enough time.

MY NEXT CHALLENGE 20 MINUTES

Read the introduction and instructions for "My Next Challenge" aloud, including the two questions. Give the girls a minute to write out their answers to the two questions, then have each girl read her answers. Give each girl a Gift Card that correlates with the next challenge she chose. At the conclusion of this exercise pray a prayer of encouragement and blessing for each girl before you dismiss.

MATERIALS NEEDED

- A copy of the *My Next Challenge* handout for each participant
- Several copies of the *Leader's Gift Cards* sheet, cut apart into individual cards. (Make at least half the number of copies as you have girls in your group.)
- Optional: A stapler, so each girl can staple her Gift Card to her sheet

Leader's Hint: Have the Gift Cards in stacks by character quality, and make enough copies of the gift cards in case more than half the girls select the same quality. As each girl reads her answers, note her character quality and prayer request on a copy of the handout to keep as your own prayer reminder. After each girl reads her answers, hand her the Gift Card corresponding to the character quality she selected, saying, "We'll pray for you, and here is one thing you can focus on to build that quality into your life." (Each Action Step is taken from the list of Action Steps in that lesson.)

TIME ALERT: Allow enough time for the girls to write their answers, so that they have a record of their desires and their prayer request. If you have more than eight girls, have each one share only her prayer request.

FOLLOW UP

Email the prayer list from the *My Next Challenge* exercise to the group after your last lesson, and encourage them to pray for one another and to keep up the connection with their Makeover Teammates.

HEAD-TO-SOUL MAKEOVER MATCHING GAME

GENEROSITY

PERSEVERANCE

THE *REALLY AMAZING*
RACE

HEAD-TO-SOUL
MAKEOVER

COURAGE

lifeswap

SELF-CONTROL

WHAT**NOT**TO**BE**

CONFIDENCE

PATIENCE

HUMILITY

CONTENTMENT

MY TOP THREE "WHAT NOT TO BE'S"

Instructions:

Remember the "What Not to Be" Quiz from Week One? In it, you discovered your top three qualities you needed to work on during this study. Circle those three qualities, and answer the following questions:

1. Now that you have finished the study, do you think the quiz results were right? Why?

2. Did you learn anything in those three lessons that helped you overcome character flaws?

Prideful Idol Humility	DON'T REPLAY THE LYRICS! Confidence
Fear or Faith **factor** Courage	**life**swap Patience
TOTAL LOSER Self-Control	*My Superficial* **SWEET 16** Contentment
Extreme **MAKEOVER** **GENEROSITY EDITION** Generosity	THE *REALLY* AMAZING **RACE** Perseverance

MY BEST FEATURE

Instructions:

Circle your best feature—the character quality in which you shine. Then answer the following questions:

1. *Why is this quality, more than any of the other qualities, your best feature?*
2. *Describe at least one thing you have done that demonstrates that quality.*

Prideful Idol Humility	DON'T REPLAY THE LYRICS! Confidence
Fear or Faith factor Courage	life**swap** Patience
TOTAL LOSER Self-Control	*My Superficial* SWEET 16 Contentment
Extreme MAKEOVER GENEROSITY EDITION Generosity	THE *REALLY* AMAZING R A C E Perseverance

I AFFIRM YOU!

AFFIRMATION OF _____ BY _____

Instructions:
Write the name of a person in your group in the first blank, and write your name in the second blank. Choose a character quality you have observed in that person's life, and write a brief description in the box, explaining why you chose that quality for her. Be specific! If you select "Patience," it's too general to say, "You are always patient with people." It's more affirming to say, "I admire how you are kind to your little brother and don't lose your temper even when he's irritating."

Prideful Idol Humility	DON'T REPLAY THE **LYRICS!** Confidence
Fear or **Faith** *factor* Courage	**life**swap Patience
TOTAL LOSER Self-Control	*My Superficial* **SWEET 16** Contentment
Extreme **MAKEOVER** **GENEROSITY EDITION** Generosity	THE *REALLY* AMAZING **R A C E** Perseverance

MY NEXT CHALLENGE

And I am sure that God who began the good work within you will keep right on helping you grow in his grace until his task within you is finally finished on that day when Jesus Christ returns.
(Philippians 1:6, TLB)

This verse says two important things you need to know about your Head-to-Soul Makeover: The first is that the "good work" of your soul makeover can only be finished by God. Without his power, you won't be able to make lasting changes. The second thing this verse says is that the process of your soul makeover will not be complete until you see Jesus face-to-face. Until then, cycle through these qualities again and again to continue working—with the power of the Holy Spirit—on your head-to-soul transformation, so that you can become more real in a fake world.

Circle the quality you want to go back to and work on again. Write the answers to the following questions on your sheet, then share them with the group.

1. Why do you want to work on this quality?

2. What specific thing do you want the group to pray about for you in this area?

Prideful Idol Humility	DON'T REPLAY THE LYRICS! Confidence
Fear or Faith factor Courage	lifeswap Patience
TOTAL LOSER Self-Control	My Superficial SWEET 16 Contentment
Extreme MAKEOVER GENEROSITY EDITION Generosity	THE REALLY AMAZING RACE Perseverance

LEADER'S GIFT CARDS

Humility

Action Step:
Go on a God Hunt

Confidence

Action Step:
Memorize Philippians 4:8

Courage

Action Step:
Turn worries into prayers

Patience

Action Step:
Get to know people who bug you

Self-Control

Action Step:
Memorize Psalm 141:3

Contentment

Action Step:
Rejoice with those who rejoice

Generosity

Action Step:
Donate your time or things

Perseverance

Action Step:
Choose a project and finish it

How *Head-to-Soul Makeover* Got Its Start

The inspiration for the *Head-to-Soul Makeover* curriculum for teen girls is Katie Brazelton's and Shelley Leith's book, *Character Makeover: 40 Days With a Life Coach to Create the Best You.* This book helps women put an end to well-worn patterns of defeat, woundedness, insecurity, unworthiness and self-centeredness by teaming with the Holy Spirit to develop eight character traits of Christlikeness.

Available in stores and online!

Character Makeover Downloadable Study Guide:
10 Small Group Sessions to Create the Best You

This downloadable study guide helps women's groups explore the critical concepts of *Character Makeover.* Each week a different television reality show is used as a metaphor to explore the strongholds that keep us from being like Christ. Group members take the weekly self-assessment quizzes to discover which aspect of that stronghold they need to deal with, then use the built-in discussion questions and activities to look into the Bible for solutions. This study combines the common situations women experience with the fun perspective that our favorite reality shows provide to make the most of the group's journey through *Character Makeover.*

The ten-week small group study for women is available as a downloadable study guide and a downloadable leader's guide from ShelleyLeith.com.

Share Your Thoughts

With the Author: Your comments will be forwarded to the author when you send them to *zauthor@zondervan.com*.

With Zondervan: Submit your review of this book by writing to *zreview@zondervan.com*.

Free Online Resources at
www.zondervan.com

Zondervan AuthorTracker: Be notified whenever your favorite authors publish new books, go on tour, or post an update about what's happening in their lives at www.zondervan.com/authortracker.

Daily Bible Verses and Devotions: Enrich your life with daily Bible verses or devotions that help you start every morning focused on God. Visit www.zondervan.com/newsletters.

Free Email Publications: Sign up for newsletters on Christian living, academic resources, church ministry, fiction, children's resources, and more. Visit www.zondervan.com/newsletters.

Zondervan Bible Search: Find and compare Bible passages in a variety of translations at www.zondervanbiblesearch.com.

Other Benefits: Register yourself to receive online benefits like coupons and special offers, or to participate in research.

ZONDERVAN®

ZONDERVAN.com/
AUTHORTRACKER
follow your favorite authors